Threading

Preface
Nida Abdullah, Chris Lee, Xinyi Li

Current institutional design education inherits and reproduces problematic systems of power and hierarchy as well as
traditional approaches to pedagogy, even as we try to change
them from the inside, the outside, and alongside the dominant,
accredited curricular, disciplinary and financial structures.

> *post-radical pedagogy* operates as a space to explore, antag-
> onize, challenge, and interrogate these forces that circum-
> scribe the pedagogical priorities and values of the studio
> and classroom—from the inertia of tradition and convention
> (historical canon and coloniality) to institutional administra-
> tive habits (grading, classes, semesters), financial pressure
> (tuition, loans), and the mandate to "make employable" (the
> market, professionalization).

Here, "post" prompts a reflection on inherited pedagogical situations and is an implicit acknowledgment of the
struggle to find a language for articulating what a radical
pedagogy and praxis in design might entail. It was within
this context that we—Nida Abdullah, Chris Lee, and Xinyi
Li, the editors of this volume—organized a series of presentations and conversations[1] across two semesters conceived
as an exploratory vehicle for uncovering ways to perceive
radical pedagogy as an expansive practice. By threading
conversations between the speakers and connecting unfin-
ished ideas, the lecture series opened up the conventional
giver-receiver relationship, making space to explore ideas
that weren't at the forefront of the discipline's institutional
spaces. These lectures were seeking and probing moments,
tentative and unrefined pedagogical attempts to name
ways of being, of knowing, of seeing.

> The first half of the lecture series was broadly organized
> around the question of race in design pedagogy, with par-
> ticular attention to the priorities of Black thinkers and mak-
> ers.[2] The second half centered around critical conceptions of
> design as work and labor, and the political tradition of print-
> ing—its history, present, and future, in relation to graphic
> design education.[3]

This publication complements the lecture series with invita-
tions from additional contributors to augment these themes.
It expands beyond the temporal limitations of the live talk
and institutional or disciplinary borders to bring a discussion on design pedagogy to a wider audience. In this project,
we have embraced a process that centers care and generative intention over an output-first production pipeline. This
intentional process has made space for building relationships together, as we have engaged with how to make sense
of complicity and negotiated grief, sadness, joy, and hope.

> "Post" doesn't mean moving past; it is a continuous search
> along the limits and boundaries of what *is* a pedagogical prac-
> tice. The following publication assembles an ongoing discourse.

1 The Post-Radical Design
Lecture Series was held
in fall 2020 and spring
2021 and documented in
the pages that follow.

2 With contributions by
Ari Melenciano, Lauren
Williams, and John
Jennings.

3 With contributions by
Silvio Lorusso, Danielle
Aubert, and Elaine
Lopez.

2

Conversation on the Terms
Dec. 2023

n i d a: The question I have is, what do we mean by witness? The word complicity comes up, but also movement through time. Complicity is there [in the chart], which I have a question about, is *complicity* part of witnessing. What do we mean by "through witnessing"? Are we complicit through our witnessing?

x i n y i: I feel like witnessing can lead to different kinds of actions depending on how you act upon what you witnessed. And what you witness needs to go through a set of procedures performatively to become actualized. If you testify, or if you do something about what you witness, it will turn into action. But also you can, you don't have to. If you don't do anything, does that kind of witness hint complicity?

n i d a: About complicity, I think witnessing is also making it real. I guess, if you're witnessing something, you're part of the reality of it. If you don't look, if you don't see, then it's not there for you. And also, I think, witnessing has this endurance kind of aspect to it, and through time.

c h r i s: I think it's also about accountability and support, corroboration... Like, a lot of the stuff that we talk about—I think we're witnessing to each other. It's kind of like proving that you're not on your own.

n i d a: I think that is a form of witnessing in a way, because it gives an experience its existence, its material. I guess in that way, there's this witnessing happening here, now.

c h r i s: I think, in witnessing. There's also something kind of oppositional. You witness to provide evidence to counter the kind of claims of the powerful or dominant narrative.

x i n y i: So in a way, sharing witness is also about creating connection, creating collective. And I think there's something about memorialization. It creates this collective memorialization, at least potentially, to collectivity, if not action, some countering force, countering narrative. When working on another project, I came across Keightley and Pickering's concept of mnemonic imagination, that memory and imagination are not separable, every time recalling something is a synthesis of remembering and imagining.

I'm interested in how witness and memory are linked, they can be both first-hand experience and media representation. Witnessing as a practice of vision, not only as a kind of seeing as a surface vision, it requires recognition and imagination of the subjectivity of the other, a sense of believing. This assemblage of individual and collective memory kind of shatters the boundary or believed autonomy of individuals, a characteristic of our neoliberal world that we also talk about in the book. We are indebted to each other to complete our subjectivities. But, is witnessing always visual?

c h r i s: There's a kind of mutual catharsis. Recognizing each other's testimony, in the face of a lot of the things that are going against us, and have no evidentiary residue.

x i n y i: I think witness also materializes differently in different kinds of spaces. If it's in a private space, like what we were saying, it's kind of like performing care work as well. But if it's in one of those more public, official, or bureaucratic spaces, witness materializes to different kinds of things that are not about personal, caring, connecting...

Another thing we've been talking about earlier is, what if we start to think about design as witness. Then it's questioning the *myth of neutrality* of design, a kind of *projection*, the idea of design is neutral, by saying design *can bear witness*—designed object, and also the process of designing.

c h r i s: The way I understand that is starting with the banal observation that, like designed things index the conditions of their making. They index ideas, attitudes, assumptions. If one is equipped to be able to unpack a designed object and understand where it came from, how it was made, etc., then the object is a kind of document that bears witness to its making.

n i d a: I agree with this but also wonder how the object and the material cannot capture some of its conditions. Maybe this refers back to embodied ways of making. Can it document things said, things unsaid and gesture? How are things witnessed outside of documentation of sorts.

x i n y i: Thinking of objects as witnessing requires a "mirror reading" of the absences.

...

c h r i s: I think schools prioritize metrics because it gives administrators something to do—a means by which they can manage pedagogy. This imperative trickles down into student pressure to perform correctly. But instead of focusing on being right, what if studio pedagogy could make space for, like, "let's just keep going until something works."

n i d a: I was thinking about the priorities and the agenda of the school and the nation to maintain basically. And the priority is to create people who can just fit into the workplace situation. We just need to keep producing. It's about hyper production.

c h r i s: It's just skill development. It's like how, but not why.

x i n y i: This also reminds me of what we've been talking about while we were working on the Printed Matter project, how colonial education is about creating these subjects. It's about creating order and education is about creating subjects that can be ordered whether it's for type or different kinds of agenda. It's never about creating chaos. This links to another word we have, *pedagogy of chaos*, as a prompt to think about.

n i d a: What is the pedagogy of chaos?

x i n y i: Teach-ins are not institutional classrooms. Students made their own classrooms that are multicentered, and graphic design is enacting on site. Is pedagogy of chaos also pedagogy of resistance against the *priorities and agendas of the school and nation*, and the *empty gesture* of school's branding?

n i d a: Student-driven actions on campuses exist outside of the boundaries of the classroom, the curriculum, the rubric, timeline etc. Often these have libraries, lectures, handouts; gatherings (a mimicking of what is known, but resistance of priorities)... this is a horizontal learning, one that is nonhierarchical. I think maybe a pedagogy of chaos is an exploring of the boundaries.

cont'd

3

Introduction
Nida Abdullah, Chris Lee, Xinyi Li

The act of witnessing is interwoven with complicity, corroboration, and contradiction. It implies endurance through time, a demand for accountability, as well as acts of collective memorialization and support that make real something that might have otherwise remained in the shadows, forgotten and not believed. Witnessing is also a way of learning and reflecting.

This book attests to how institutions, design, and designed things are implicated in maintaining colonial capitalist world systems. It reflects, critiques, and laments what it means to teach and to design today. Using design as a lens to witness the mechanisms at play in maintaining existing orders as well as material conditions of representation and erasure, of rage and chaos, the book asks: How does design give form to social fiction? How does design and the professionalization of design schooling maintain the priorities of nations and capital? What do designers make as laborers when they are implicated in systems of inertia? How do the expectations of mainstream pedagogy, with its baggage of paternalism and professionalization, put limits on radical potentials?

The contributions in the following pages come from educators and practitioners who address these questions through pedagogical praxis and design practices that center learning.[4] With excerpts from lectures and conversations, essays, and interviews, this book emerged as a pedagogy over several years. The reader will note that this text is marked by date subheadings to reflect the extended period over which it was developed and written—a commitment, in form if nothing else, to the contingency that a critical orientation toward knowledge production ought to abide. The slowness of the process allows the publication to witness the unfolding chains of events, and expand contexts of discussions. The result presents not a single prognosis, but multiple voices and perspectives organized into three sections: *Critiquing*, *Making*, and *Teaching*, with the editors' *Threading* to highlight their resonances.

The *Threading* section of this book also includes a fold-out that maps the ways the book's themes resonate with one another. This section is akin to an index, presenting themes that emerge from our doubts about inherited pedagogical priorities, values, and their circumstances. In search of a language, the editors performed slower, more intimate readings of the texts over time, moving closer to them, developing relationships between them, and drawing out threads in a way that conventional keyword-based indexing could not. The terms with excerpts are meant to serve as prompts rather than as a complete directory. *Threading* provides multiple points of entry and divergence, prompting readers to engage with the content through various lenses and make their own connections. With excerpts exemplifying the themes, this section may be read as a standalone piece. Pithy labels provide only one way of ordering, and can't contain all the leakages of the work. The reader will find annotations in the marginalia, set in this red.

The *Critiquing* section questions the banal assumptions that overcode designing and design. Starting with a conversation between Lauren Williams and John Jennings—two designers and intellectuals whose thinking, enacted through their creative work and writing, both expose the gaps in the normative priorities of the discipline and show possible critical paths beyond these. Their conversation, titled "Design, Race and Speculation: From Horror to the Specter of Black Liberation," explores their respective practices through the speculative dimensions of design,

4   In these sections, readers may note differences in the contributors' annotative approaches and spellings. As editors, we made the decision to keep these differences and highlight academic traces while acknowledging that we are products of various educational contexts.

4

c h r i s: Probably the most minimum definition of the pedagogy of chaos would be it's the one that doesn't have measurable outcomes, right? The school generates/graduates those who can comply with essentially commercial orders, right? So like "use a grid" is not an aesthetic injunction, it's a managerial one. Because the grid is a part of this loosely constructed set of normative values in design. The grid is the thing that if you align to it, it looks designed. So using a grid is ultimately a kind of performative design-y virtue signaling. Operationally grid systems help to coordinate and distribute the labor of creating different sections of a big book, or website, etc. to a team of designers and have them do something separately but coherently. The grid enables multiple simultaneous projections of some spatial/visual intent across many workspaces and actuates the industrialization of designing.

n i d a: Is the grid a kind of mechanism of maintenance? In that it is a way to keep things ordered and the same?

x i n y i: Grid as a mechanism of maintenance, is this claiming too much responsibility on design? Grid on paper vs grid in cities speaks to different senses of responsibility. In P.R.China "grid-person" is a type of temporary worker who enacts "grid-style social management" and community governance, especially during zero-covid, It's human surveillance.

n i d a: I think that the grid is like a *social fiction*, this idea of good design or order, making something good that gets projected and is perpetually handed down.

This idea of *mechanisms of maintenance*, it seems like it overlaps with social fiction. The more I think about it.. How does something become a mechanism of maintenance? So something like race is a mechanism of maintenance, is it not? So it's a social fiction. Well, or maybe social fictions are upheld by mechanisms of maintenance.

c h r i s: This is with academia more broadly, but especially with creative fields: a teacher saying this is "right" or "wrong" doesn't really have any solid foundation except for suggesting "this is how it's always been done." So with this sort of contestability, being

charismatic or being mean, turns out to be a way to back up the assumptions of one's argument.

And so I'm just going back to another term here, *pedagogy of forgiveness*. I think it's the antidote, where teachers let go of having to be right, or having to be the smartest person in the room in order to be a teacher.

n i d a: I think pedagogy of forgiveness implies a hierarchical situation, where one person is holding more power over another or over an object. I wonder if there are other ways to name this. Maybe something softer or more ongoing.

...

n i d a: To *horizontal learning*, I guess I'm wondering about this like teacher-learner relationship, or dynamic? Is it always a teaching hierarchy? Or can it be all learner, learner, learner, or all teacher, teacher? Does it have to be like a giver-receiver relationship? Is this also a kind of pedagogy of chaos? An exploring of the boundaries?

x i n y i: On horizontal learning space and linking back to grading or evaluation earlier, I'm also thinking about how education is viewed as something as scarcity. it's not available to everyone, at least in traditional elite institutional settings. So like grading, having criteria and different kinds of evaluative things creates hierarchies among people, because it's a selective mechanism. Not everybody gets through the system, and I feel that connects to the ugliness of eugenics. What is the process of filtering and selecting? And what is this filtering and selecting system doing? If this horizontal learning frees the hierarchy, how do we think of teaching outside of the scarcity mode and as something for all?

n i d a: I think also in evaluation and grading, it's like you have to prove that something happened, that there was learning. I think we all know this. But just sitting in a space together, there is some kind of transfer. Of course, not according to the priorities of the school, in their eyes, there has to be something measurable because well, they are a business, and they have to prove that they did something, like proof of knowledge transfer, or proof of learning.

x i n y i: But if we consider the promises of design schools, at least in more elite institutions,

goes beyond commercial design. professionalism is not the only thing that schools try to brand themselves. They want to have an image of a progressive school, and then they are trying to say to the students that the curriculum also engages with these other aspects of things. I think there are a lot of conflicts in building that image and the rest of the criteria in the inner processes of actually running the program.

c h r i s: But I think a lot of the problems or the tensions that we come up against in teaching come from somebody trying to rationalize curriculum and pedagogy—to streamline it in such a way that everybody's outcomes are legible, and how learning outcomes and assignments are aligned in ways that are rational and legible, so that from an overview perspective of an administrator's desk, one can see trends and make policy decisions based on these.

Here is where that lesson of the scientific forests and the emergence of rational forestry management is instructive. The people who tried to make rational forests so that they can commercialize tree harvesting, designed the forests to make them legible. That is, the trees were planted in neat rows, and they were all numbered to correspond to a line on a spreadsheet. But the designers of these forests, prioritizing commercial rationality, didn't account for the complexity of forest ecosystems and the forests began failing after one or two harvests. What they missed in their design was, among other things, the role of insects and deer shit—all these things they couldn't register or predict or model into their scheme but are actually critical to the health of the forest ecosystem. It makes beautiful sense to the administrator from the comfort of their bureau, but it doesn't make sense on the ground.

x i n y i: this connects to our first term, *bureaucratization* — colonialism as a bureaucratization of inequality. the bureaucratization of teaching, reduces the performance in the classroom, the fields, to the administrative desks. I thought it's funny when I saw this Dunhuang tenth-century Buddhist manuscript illustrating the ten stages that a soul passes through following death, and how the ten "Kings of Hell seated behind their administrative desks, wearing offi cial robes and hats in judgment."

5

cont'd

race, and time. Together, they cast design as a mechanism for generating and maintaining oppression, but also as a tool for producing representations that name and oppose it. Fermentation, transcendence, and the weaponization of Black laughter are just a few of the concepts and forms they actuate to this end. The entanglement of notions for both Williams and Jennings is at once banal and charged with rage and monstrous horror, Yet, their work responds to the assertion that all organizing is a form of science fiction that envisions many other socially just worlds.[5]

Their exchange is followed by an interview with Williams, who elaborates on her practice and explores design's potential function beyond service to capital and its participation in reproducing racism through technology, and addresses the fraught choice between visibility and invisibility, or perhaps in more charged terms, recognition and evasion. She also reflects on the deeply techno-solutionist tendencies of speculative design, while considering futuring as an organizing tool toward the abolition of police and prisons.

The design studies scholar Ahmed Ansari contributes an essay that includes many rich layers of comparison between restructuring the Single National Curriculum in Pakistan and delinking in decolonial theories, reflecting on design education in Pakistan and the United States. His text recognizes culture and design as non-essentializable sites of continuous change that exceed binary configurations like modernity vs. tradition, Occident vs. Orient, white vs. brown, etc., and poignantly disabuses "decolonization"—or at least its US-American-inflected meaning—of its certainties. Ansari shakes the parochial Western framing of so many other concepts endemic to North/West design discourse and its embarrassment of dubious assumptions.

The *Making* section offers reflections on what designers make and how they connect with systems of production. It opens with a conversation between two dedicated design educators who concluded the original lecture series. In "The Joy and Politics of Printing," a title adapted from Danielle Aubert's book on the Detroit Printing Co-op, Aubert and Elaine Lopez converse about precisely that: Lopez discusses the RISO printer's function as a vehicle for a pedagogy that conditions the studio as a place of generosity, ease, and forgiveness. She discusses how the machine—its idiosyncrasies, malfunctions, and the ways that users adapt to it—enables the discussion of radical pedagogies, non-Western perspectives, and forms of self-care that inspire form-making and self-publishing about identity, culture, and social issues. Aubert's contribution explores a long and rich history of leftists working as printers. As a relatively accessible means of production, she argues, the printing press continues to inspire designers, who see it as having the potential to subvert the kind of alienation endemic to the discipline. Printing imbricates cognitive and manual labor; it demands attention to craft, and as a consequence can bring pleasure to those who engage with it. Yet, she asks, what are the limits and potentials of printing as a political act? What is a revolutionary printer today?

The interview that follows allows us to think further about the professionalization of labor and the values of craft. Does finding joy in one's labor mitigate the alienation of wage for work? Can the printer/press itself become a kind of classroom where collective labor and learning are horizontally organized for expanding, rather than simply transferring, knowledge and skill? What is the designer/printer's relationship to machines and tools? What can be learned from an appreciation of craft and materiality? What are the political and disciplinary—that is, the labor-organizational—consequences of insisting on the value of these elements?

5   See Walidah Imarisha, and Adrienne Maree Brown, editors. *Octavia's Brood: Science Fiction Stories from Social Justice Movements*. AK Press, 2015.

n i d a: And this conversation is kinda getting me down, I feel sad. If all these things exist and all these things we come up against, Where is the space where I fit, or why am I doing this? You know?

c h r i s: These acts of resistance tend not to have legible outcomes, right? The solutionist habits of designers and educators excludes negation, passivity, not enacting the violence of institutions. But I think what this suggests is that the normal activities are actually really harmful. Not doing harm means not doing those things.

x i n y i: *Slowness* is like these other kinds of performances intentionally under the radar. Isn't this undoing or un-maintaining? Slowing down is to stop following the mechanisms of maintenance.

n i d a: I have this image of *undoing*, how you put a wrench in the machine. And I was like, what about a cloggy pedagogy like you're clogging the toilet or like clogging the machine, how do you? What is your stuck pedagogy? I was listening to your analogy Chris, with the trees and the spreadsheet, when the forest dies, or whatever they don't see the slow growth of things, either. Things have to happen quickly, or the smallest change is not noticed because it's not big enough.

x i n y i: Continuing with the forest analogy, I'm also thinking about mushroom foraging in the forest. If someone is only extractive, they can use whatever tool to pick up the fungi. If it's metal, it's going to shock the mycelium system, and it will stop fruiting the next year. But if you use a wooden stick, or a bamboo one, that's a natural material, you're preserving the mycelia to become fruitful again next year. This is like the harsh teacher, the cold, metal kind of tool. It might be productive at first, but it's not creating a long-term caring, more joyful way of learning, maintaining curiosity, and nurturing a practice in a sustainable way.

...

c h r i s: Classes taught in ways that are damaging... this kind of teaching also teaches abusiveness as the way to settle contestable normative values within the practice.

n i d a: Yes, and it's the behavior that gets handed down. As you move out from the classroom, maybe as somebody in a position of power, not only is the content

reproduced but so is the harmful behavior.

c h r i s: It's like when someone gets upset about kerning or something. Now, I'm just like, "Are you OK? Did somebody die?"

x i n y i: It's reminding me of what Silvio has been talking about. By having the same value a community can be created, you feel like belonging to a kind of community of practice, practitioners.

n i d a: What does it mean to belong to this community, I wonder.

c h r i s: Is belonging legitimacy? Do those two words, legible and legitimate, connect?

n i d a: The world certainly thinks the certificate matters for recognition. And I feel to belong to the community, you have to be recognized in some way.

x i n y i: Certificates, and these terms, standards, are also *social fiction*. People have agreed upon the acceptance of them as the standards. That's a projection of ideas. I'm about to connect to what you're saying, Chris. Nida, you were saying earlier how the conversation is such a bummer, but when you were speaking about the pedagogy of clog you were laughing. And, Chris, when you were speaking about how you were freaks of the school you were also laughing. And I wonder if that is a space where we can find joy within the space of practice, within the space of pedagogy. When we're not following a top-down order and trying to invent something.

c h r i s: And maybe that's the point of this book, or this project too. Maybe design school is half about design, and half about learning how to be or practicing being in ways that resist.

x i n y i: This brings back how we started this conversation, about how witnessing is also a way of creating connection and creating space for each other. Perhaps the different contributions in this book, and us, we're also kind of using the book as space to witness what's been brought up in the content of the contributions.

n i d a: Oh, I agree. This idea of school, design school, isn't just about designing. I do think it's about practicing a lot, practicing being, and practicing being human or whatever, but practicing what it means to relate to one another, practicing different kinds of things.

x i n y i: I like how we are saying, schooling it's also learning a way of being, or ways of being. I'm looking at a note here on slowness.

It's a question: is there a slow that is not outcome-oriented? I think learning to be slowly is not actually slowness, it's not delaying the outcome that arrives eventually. The slowness is actually just about the process of ongoingness.

n i d a: I was thinking about slowness, too. Slowness is a way of being. It's not about the thing though. It's about the time or the movement or the process of movement, meaning, not not moving. Yeah, not about slowing down how you get to a place or a thing, but just being, a way of being slow.

I wonder, too, if there is slowness as ways of knowing. I think there's also a lot of urgency in having to know everything right now. And being an expert on it. But that's just not possible. What does it mean to understand or comprehend? Can we process slowly? Can we embody slowness?

Maybe pedagogy of chaos is slowness, since we can't immediately see its order in how it expands and unfolds. Maybe the pedagogy of clog is also slowness and congested in its unevenness.

x i n y i: Oh, and it's also like a word in parentheses we have here. It's intentional slowness and not just the inertia kind of slowness. That's two types of slowness. One is, inertia, it's kind of passively slow, gripped by other mechanisms of maintenance. The other one is intentionally slow.

c h r i s: I think one of the things that's radical about slowness in the school context is, you can think about impact besides the typical timeframe of delivering a workshop, a lesson, an assignment, a semester. But if you consider the longer-term impact that goes beyond even graduation, where the outcome is not gonna be measured or legible to the institution, that tends to not be prioritized.

n i d a: Yeah and there are things that happen outside of these parameters, what it was, what it did and who it touched, how it happened or anything, it's not legible. And the effects of this can emerge many years after the initial school encounter.

c h r i s: There's these different frequencies, or wavelengths of impact. The ones that are prioritized in the curriculum are the ones we might call "higher frequency." They're more legible, than the lower, deeper ones, the slower ones.

7

The designer and educator Kelly Walters introduces her remixing and remaking practice, which focuses on how print materials from Black entertainment (i.e., leaflets, playbills, and promotional signage) witness the evolution of what she refers to as "racial labeling." These graphic design artifacts function as both mechanisms of maintenance that reinforce the projection of racial labels, and as evidence of the ways in which Black people "began to assert greater authority over how they chose to be identified" Through activating racial stereotypes found in museum collections and archives, Walters asks: "How have Black images been shaped through the lens of whiteness? How do archives perpetuate and maintain racial tropes and stereotypes? How can design be used to create counternarratives that disrupt demeaning depictions?" Walters likens her remaking process of freestyling and remixing to that of sampling in hip-hop: a radical act of being, of "going to the root or origin; fundamental." This actuates a reflexive process to cultivate social consciousness about the impact and effects of representation.

Based on ethnographic short stories of lived experiences in design schools, Hayfaa Chalabi and Maya Ober, two design educators (based in Europe at the time of the lecture series), share reflections on the challenges and struggles of institutional work. Reflecting on the discrepancy between the well-meaning promises of educational institutions and the sometimes traumatic realities of students' experiences, Chalabi and Ober lament how poorly defined efforts at decolonization are often hoisted on students, activists, and POC faculty as an additional, uncompensated burden. The examples of institutional efforts to "decolonize" appear as cosmetic changes and demonstrate the academic system's propensity to maintain its coloniality. If practicing decolonial thinking within the institution is unproductive, even perhaps impossible, what is to be done? Chalabi and Ober challenge us to consider abandoning performative forms of inclusion and superficial one-off gestures, and commit in word and deed to ontological ones.

The contributions in the *Teaching* section engage with pedagogical issues from the perspective of teachers locked into institutional curricula, and turn to the potentialities of actions that challenge and undo dominant orders.

Writing from a North American institutional context, Uzma Z. Rizvi reminds us that continuing service to institutions "without undoing these forms, systems, and policies that hold racist, classist, heteropatriarchal ways of doing" makes us complicit in the maintenance of the settler-colonial system. She argues that the colonial academy subordinates service and care work as having lesser value "in order to ensure that those most likely to launch institutional critique are the ones who want to stay far away from it." Rizvi asks how to approach a reevaluation of service and an understanding of the transformative power of service, not for the neoliberal university but for "generations of bodies moving through these spaces [for whom] we are working to ensure a safe passage."

Silvio Lorusso's provocative talk entitled "Design and Disillusion: A Starter Pack," opened up his research on the apparent disillusion permeating the design field. Lorusso looks at self-deprecating memes and considers how we navigate generational resentment and confront the soul-crushing nature of everyday life within creative industries. His insights then, as always, hold up to what we might call in our field "a crystal clear mirror" through which to conduct a sobering examination of the vain illusions that design (education) regularly dresses itself in.

We followed up with Lorusso in an interview to dig deeper into the role of design and its promises. Distinguishing design from designers; interrogating designers' agency and the degree to which design has been attributed more responsibility

8

than it can actually claim; considering professionalization, craft, and chaos... we follow this erudite witness who identifies design's delusions, and whose thought corroborates with clarity what many of us may only experience as a vague feeling of disillusionment.

In sum, these texts contemplate the conflicting expectations, promises, and realities of an engagement with graphic design education and practice. Moving between a sense of sadness and futility while also finding moments of light and camaraderie, our hope as editors is that these contributors' work will help the reader to articulate and further develop their own ways of understanding and addressing the predicament of being a design student, educator, and practitioner.

Threading critiquing, making, teaching

10

launch institutional critique are the ones who want to stay far away from it and maintain themselves as disaffected.
Essay, Uzma Z. Rizvi

One can't help but think of colonialism and its extractive relationship with cultures, practices, and lifeways rooted in places far from the imperial metropoles.
Essay, Maya Ober and Hayfaa Chalabi

cosmetic change / empty gestures

None of these structural features seem to have changed throughout Imran Khan's tenure, which has sought to remake the content of education while leaving its larger structural and infrastructural problems untouched.
Essay, Ahmed Ansari

I'm not saying that I think Black people have been passively waiting over time to be delivered from injustice, but instead that historically, the trend has been for the nation as a whole to admonish Black people for being patient, for making demands in a particular way that's palatable and acceptable, and for accepting performative gestures like the street scale mural that you see in the background here, instead of a response to the demands they're actually asking for.
Lecture, Lauren Williams

Instead of a deeper, critical engagement with Western canons, the underpinning sociopolitics of the human-made world, and the complicity of academic institutions in upholding colonial and patriarchal epistemologies, design schools prefer more cosmetic changes. "Inclusivity," for instance, has become a buzzword in Western design institutions. Its mobilization echoes the way that the British Empire "included'" colonized subjects in its colonial administration. Design schools fall into the trap of tokenism in hiring practices, following an additive approach to satisfy agitators' demands. However, these measures only sustain existing power structures, "offsetting demands for radical systemic change" (Decolonizing Design 2018). The result is that these faculty often find themselves isolated in their relative specialness.

     ...

Decolonization remains, as such, an empty buzzword, since the institutions are apparently unable to genuinely engage in forms of transformative work and knowledge production— as inferred by the grievances sketched out above—which are crucial to decolonization (Bhambra 2018).
Essay, Maya Ober and Hayfaa Chalabi

erasure

see projection (pg. 16); see capitalism (pg. 30)

normative evaluation

There is often a vast discrepancy between the kind of education institutions outwardly present in their mission statements and students' lived reality once inside.
Essay, Maya Ober and Hayfaa Chalabi

In very much the same way, we find those bodies who do the work of maintenance of academic process are particular (often BIPOC and women), and as such, this work is seen as having lesser value. And so, we are taught our academic value systems based on these hierarchies of colonial privilege.
Essay, Uzma Z. Rizvi

see accountability / complicity (pg. 12)

accountability / complicity

Does that designer creating work around their race make some quality of their identity more consumable, palatable, or profitable for the machine of racial capitalism or neoliberalism in the process? Are they (inadvertently or not) using the tools of a racist patriarchy to prop up that racist patriarchy?

Interview, Lauren Williams pg.57

Instead of accountability toward violent educational systems that privilege certain voices over others, these institutions decide to put the labor of deconstructing oppressive histories on the systemically marginalized.

...pg.108

While we acknowledge and address unjust power structures in the educational institution, we believe our positions as teachers inside the classroom remain complicit in reproducing sometimes violent, vertical learning experiences. We are faced with our own emotional exhaustion every time we need to explain white innocence, white saviorism, and/or unpack any student work that reproduces problematic narratives

Essay, Maya Ober and Hayfaa Chalabi pg.113

If service is, indeed, faculty labor to keep the machine going, then how do we contend with the complicity of maintaining a system that we may not agree with, that is, a colonial system? Isn't that exactly what it means to be complicit in maintaining the violent structures of the academy? If we continue to work for the academic-industrial complex, without undoing these forms, systems, and policies that uphold racist, classist, heteropatriarchal ways of doing, we are, in fact, complicit in the maintenance of the settler-colonial system. This essay takes its cue from this moment and presents an analysis of service that takes into account the ways by which service is proffered, and the ways by which we may reorient those bureaucracies in the service of decolonization.

Essay, Uzma Z. Rizvi pg.119

see inbetweener (pg. 31); see also responsibilization of design (pg. 26)

(myth of) neutrality
(of design/mechanisms of maintenance)

More troubling is that immigrant designers and international students in the North/West, as well as local ones in the South/East, continue to find US-centric vocabularies useful and utilize them unproblematically—it is particularly disheartening to see students in the US show projects that continue to reify tired old tropes since this indicates that design faculty in the US are not doing the work of getting international students to critically interrogate their own subject positions and home contexts.

Essay, Ahmed Ansari pg.73

It's important to state that most of my work rests on an understanding that race is something that has been designed. And by that, I mean, it has been deliberately crafted and imbued with a set of functions and features, most of which I would argue concern its capacity to keep people organized and oppressed in the ways that capitalism requires to extract and hoard wealth.

Lecture, Lauren Williams pg.34

This is the orientation I bring to classrooms. Most of the time, that has meant somewhat surreptitiously trying to counter some degree of what I know is the mainstream pedagogy surrounding me, to which students have already been indoctrinated. That has meant tweaking a thesis studio to reinforce the notion that we are all bringing some semblance of our positioning in the world (identity, geography, beliefs) to whatever we design; driving home the myth of "neutrality."

Interview, Lauren Williams pg.53

The graduate show we attended in October reflected a reality of the design-school-as-factory, wherein isolated, dominant, value-free, apolitical design is reproduced mechanically in great volumes.
Essay, Maya Ober and Hayfaa Chalabi   pg.112

see mechanisms of maintenance (pg. 10)

schooling / university

the priorities/agenda of the school and nation

What's more, there is a great disparity in the quality of teachers, administration, and infrastructure between all three systems, and they suffer from a disconnect between curricula and social-cultural realities when it comes to who is allowed to attend school (particularly along the lines of gender difference), who learns and find themselves reflected in their education (language, ethnicity, and culture), and who can attend what kind of school (class).   pg.65

...

[...] colonial authorities in the early-mid nineteenth century did indeed institute the first universities, where Anglophone education was intended to create a new class of local bureaucrats hailing largely from the existing upper castes and classes, and receiving great support from leading Indian intellectuals and educational reformers of the day [...]
Essay, Ahmed Ansari   pg.65

I would like to argue that these values are also a part of the false logic and consciousness perpetuated by the settler-colonial academy in order to ensure that those most likely to launch institutional critique are the ones who want to stay far away from it and maintain themselves as disaffected.
Essay, Uzma Z. Rizvi   pg.120

expectations of schooling / mainstream pedagogy / paternalistic baggage

Pedagogically, there was a strain of the (colonial?) "strict schoolmaster"-style of teaching that seems to have gone out of fashion in the last few decades in US academia, although it certainly did exist there too, judging from the horror stories one hears from students of Paul Rand: stern and inaccessible demeanors, an emphasis on discipline and punishment through tight deadlines and high standards, critique styles largely focusing on faults and frailties and very little on what students do well, a certain wariness of breaking convention or departing from instructor expectations, and a constant reinforcement of the image of the instructor as "the master" in a master-apprentice system.
Essay, Ahmed Ansari   pg.68

So, my operative mode tends to be a stubbornly strategic misuse of the practice, particularly in classrooms where pedagogy prioritizes preparing students for industry.
Interview, Lauren Williams   pg.53

I'd like to consider riso printing as a graphic design experience that has the potential to help students expand their worldview and liberate themselves from some of the expectations and stresses that studying graphic design currently carries.
...   pg.78
I think it's very easy to look at the amazing projects that come out of programs, but not consider the mental and physical tolls they take on students.
...   pg.78
They would say, "Wow, I'm just so stressed out all the time with other classes that I never knew that learning could be fun, or that making could just be recycling things and going against all of this stuff that we are taught as designers is not okay: you need to make

fresh products for every class, it all needs to be original, and it all needs to be perfect and marketable and how's it going to look in your portfolio."
Lecture, Elaine Lopez

pg.80

see mechanisms of maintenance (pg. 10)

promise of design schools

Every semester we are confronted with well-intentioned student projects that seek to engage with pressing contemporary social and environmental justice struggles, explore cross-cultural collaborations, and expand the understanding of design beyond its horizons of problem-solving and service provision. Students rarely take into account their respective positionalities in relation to the subject matter. Their works often lack a critical reflection on their "design-politics," a term elaborated by design researcher and anthropologist Mahmoud Keshavarz to emphasize the interconnectedness of these two fields of knowledge (Keshavarz 2020).

...
pg.106

Many design programs across Europe have started promoting themselves as intellectual sanctuaries wherein students can explore questions of decolonization and foster engagements with feminist and Indigenous practices and knowledges. Regretfully, the promise of facilitating such work often remains just that, because the teaching staff lack the tools, knowledge, resources, time, and sometimes the will to engage meaningfully with, say, depatriarchalizing and decolonizing their educational programs.

...
pg.106

There is often a vast discrepancy between the kind of education institutions outwardly present in their mission statements and students' lived reality once inside.
Essay, Maya Ober and Hayfaa Chalabi

pg.109

On the left, you see the theoretical self-aggrandizing and self-empowering view of designers [designers can take hold of, dismantle, and rewire some of the abusive structures of capital by manipulating an interplay of physical contours that are also expressing limits, capacities, and values), and then on the right, the most concrete daily reality. .
Lecture, Silvio Lorusso

pg.131

see revolutionary (pg. 17); see empty gesture (pg. 11); see inertia (pg. 15)

pedagogy...
of chaos

I feel like most skills in design have huge learning curves. Think about After Effects, coding, and Cinema 4D. But with Riso printing, I was able to take images that I already had on my computer and turn them into beautiful prints in just a few minutes.
Lecture, Elaine Lopez

pg.79

These restrictions give students some parameters that help narrow down the possibilities of what to make. Some specific limitations in Riso printing include the weight, texture, and size of the paper that can be printed on, the particular colors you have access to, and the misregistration that is likely to occur from print to print. These factors will undoubtedly influence what is produced, but that is part of the fun.
Interview, Elaine Lopez

pg.92

Craft shouldn't be deceptively pre-digital, but consciously post-digital, that is, critical of digital technology and its guiding ideologies. It should be embedded in the present time and reshuffle notions of the cutting edge and passé: a lot of hi-tech software doesn't allow you to develop a craft, only to become a pro-user dependent on the tool.

...
pg.140

A pedagogy of chaos understands design as witchcraft: design is an elastic magic circle wherein constant negotiation takes place. What is order? What's entropy? Who decides what's what?

14 ...
pg.141

A pedagogy of chaos is, therefore, also able to tactically shrink the magic circle, because it understands that conceptual inclusion comes at a cost: it takes time and energy.

Finally, a pedagogy of chaos questions the covert, conservative attitude implied by the very notion of order. Not only does order appear provisional and brittle, it also limits design's projective potential. Order is the past casting its shadow; it is an instrument of what philosopher Tony Fry calls "defuturing."
Interview, Silvio Lorusso   pg.141

---

of forgiveness

How generous is the Riso, right? It prints a ton of copies very quickly. It's also forgiving— sometimes the mistakes that come out are actually more beautiful than what you intended.
...   pg.79
I encourage students to make from a place of joy and self-discovery without worrying too much about perfection.
Lecture, Elaine Lopez   pg.79

---

of resistance

see horizontal (pg. 19)

---

time

When I'm talking about racism or working through projects where racism is the question, I'm often thinking about histories that are inherited. But then, at the same time, a lot of my work is looking at how we produce futures without racism, for example, how we draw that future closer together with our present reality and with those histories we've inherited.
Lecture, Lauren Williams   pg.35

And if there is no mass movement, the more it can participate in laying the groundwork for those moments when the spark does come, the more effective it can be.
...   pg.81
It takes a long time for movements to build. It's up and down.
Lecture, Danielle Aubert   pg.85

These songs are classics and hold so much meaning across multiple generations in the Black and African American communities. For me, just hearing the first three bars of any of these songs situates me in a Black space, place, and time.
Essay, Kelly Walters   pg.100

---

inertia (waiting)

I'm thinking about Black rage as a product of chronic waiting.   pg.37
...
I'm thinking about waiting for something that is delayed or waiting for something that's past due. I think about Black rage as a product of repeated racism over time.
Lecture, Lauren Williams   pg.37

Somebody gets out at the end of it, but you don't know. It's not going to be you. It might not be me, but maybe it will be my son. Maybe it'll be his son. These systems were put in place a long time ago and they are extremely well-designed. I kind of admire their design— stereotypes function very well.
Lecture, John Jennings   pg.50

see material condition of Black rage (pg. 24); see speculation (pg. 16)

(intentional) slowness

15

speculation / imagination

How might we think of sustainability in a country where catastrophic climate change is not speculation but imminent reality, and where public infrastructure to cope with the latter is nonexistent and unlikely to be built?
Essay, Ahmed Ansari

Still, compelling storytelling—some of which employs speculative fiction and designed objects—can be powerful. Seeing, holding, turning over, or standing within tangibly different worlds—as facilitated by design mediums—can help people see their own realities in a new light, understand urgencies and pitfalls more viscerally, and grasp our role in seemingly intangible futures in an uncanny way.
...

I've struggled, in part, because I'm afraid of concretizing them as fixed narratives—I want them to live as provocations, to be used to generate other stories, as jumping-off points, as points for conversation, not as predictions about alternative worlds.
...

Both of these settings—which asked others to interpret the objects for themselves—highlighted the fact that misreads of the artifacts were also telling and valuable in their own way.
Interview, Lauren Williams

How do we emphasize or speculate on our understanding of Black identities?
Essay, Kelly Walters

He says that it's not so much creating debate as it is about reducing debate to a very narrow idea of what debate is, specifically, press releases, short semi-critical interviews, and so on. So instead of fostering debate, we have a narrowing down of what debate means.
Lecture, Silvio Lorusso

speculation of social fictions

So, when I work through design, I'm often making diegetic prototypes that question the construct of race, or bend our conception of time in some way, like proposing a different kind of future, or a different understanding of race or racism. For me, design is only one way that I arrive at these questions about how oppression works and why, and what can be done about it.
Lecture, Lauren Williams

see projection (pg. 16) ; see reassembling (pg. 25)

projection
of social fictions / stereotype / race

Ironically, these images illustrate a picture of Pakistan that mirrors the kinds of images of "authentic" Islamicate culture and society that have so dominated the imaginaries of the Anglo-European world and circulated in the West—images that the postcolonial scholar Edward Said famously critiqued in his book, Orientalism[...]
...

[...] the very US-centric language and conceptual framings of decolonisation, with their particular emphasis on very US-specific understandings of race, culture, indigeneity, etc., have a tendency to travel quickly over global circuits of information exchange and dominate local understandings.
Essay, Ahmed Ansari

Race is the ultimate "diegetic prototype."
...

When I say diegetic prototype, what I mean is an object or experience, usually a technological one, that lives in a fictional world. Diegesis is a term that comes from film. I find myself often working through producing diegetic prototypes as a way to ask the questions I'm exploring in my research or to push on these definitions of race as something that is real.

...

Because we can work with form, we can work with materiality, and we can construct these prototypes that I mentioned in the beginning. We can challenge or unsettle the notion of race as something real in the world.

Lecture, Lauren Williams

"The problem of the twentieth century is a problem with the color line," wrote W.E.B. DuBois in 1903. My only thing about this is that he wasn't thinking far enough into it. I guess he thought that by the twenty-first century, this wouldn't be an issue, but some things like racism are really well designed. That's one of the things I admire about race and stereotypes in general. One of my favorite quotes about race is from Charles W. Mills's the Racial Contract, where he posits race as a kind of virtual reality, as a construct itself. This idea of the projection of race onto unwanted people is really interesting

Lecture, John Jennings

I did, however, come to understand that design—broadly interpreted as manipulating materials, forms, and spaces to shape an experience—paired with a critical orientation and a deeper political foundation, could also offer a set of tools for asking crucial questions about why social fictions like racism prevail, why capitalism is so hard to change, and why we continue to distribute power so unevenly. Beyond that, I came to understand it as a tool for "imagining otherwise," to borrow from Christina Sharpe.

Interview, Lauren Williams

How have Black images been shaped through the lens of whiteness?

Essay, Kelly Walters

revolutionary

I can imagine it and I can design it and make it seem real, but it is literally going to require revolutions. And that is not a designed act. That's a completely different set of actions.

Lecture, Lauren Williams

If the Detroit Printing Co-op was a radical print workshop, which I think it was, there are some questions we can ask from that. What made it radical? Was it the things they printed? Was it their internal structure? Was it the movements they were a part of? And then, on the other hand, we can ask: what would a radical print shop look like today?

...

I'm interested in thinking through is in fact revolution.

...

To come back to the revolutionary potential of printing, I think that one way to think about it is that the more closely it can be connected to a mass movement the better, or the more revolutionary, it can be. And if there is no mass movement, the more it can participate in laying the groundwork for those moments when the spark does come, the more effective it can be.

...

Another concrete way to maximize the revolutionary potential of a printing practice is to connect as much as possible to mass movements, or to movements that are laying the groundwork for mass movements.

...

I think the best way to be a revolutionary printer is to be committed to being a revolutionary.

Whatever that might mean. And that is not an easy task, but it's achievable, I think. It involves finding other leftists, socialists, radicals, and progressives doing this work around you. It could mean going to meetings of groups in your area, seeing who's organizing, joining a union, forming a union, forming a co-op, supporting a strike. Maybe it's navigating the nonprofit industrial complex and identifying who's effective, who's actually challenging systems of power, and who's preventing things from moving forward and trying to slow things down—who's getting in the way.
Lecture, Danielle Aubert

pg.85

Another example comes from Enzo Mari, a utopian. He was an artist before, and he became a designer because he believed that art didn't produce the transformational change needed to change the world. But then, after a decade or two of work, he started to doubt that the designer was the center of this transformational change. So he published an advert in a big Italian design magazine in which he was desperately seeking an entrepreneur, highlighting the fact that the central figure of transformational change within companies and firms is the entrepreneur. So he was sort of disillusioned in this sense, with centrality and hierarchy.
Lecture, Silvio Lorusso

pg.127

Most activist design faces the same problem: it is stuck in the humanistic, declarative register of outrage. Its job is to assert what's wrong and give form to such assertions. When internet users do more or less the same thing that activist designers do, for instance, by posting a black square on their Instagram profiles, we become aware of the dilution of design into communication at large.
Interview, Silvio Lorusso

pg.136

unmaintain / undoing

We're really good at actually updating things. Every time you look around, a new app for your phone is updating itself. So I think we should probably rethink how we think about racial identity.
Lecture, John Jennings

pg.40

What does it mean to undo in the context of the institute (here being used to gloss the university, holding within it the system and technologies of settler coloniality), within spaces of creativity, experimentation, and project-oriented pedagogies? What precisely are we looking to undo, and in the service of what? And perhaps more pragmatically, what comes after we are undone?

...

pg.118

Service, then, is not work done only to maintain curricular functions, but rather, an ethic that informs all ways of being such that harm is not replicated. That is what must be valued.

...

pg.121

Do not be mistaken: it is not the neoliberal university that we are out to protect and save, it is the generations of bodies moving through these spaces that we are working to ensure a safe passage.
Essay, Uzma Z. Rizvi

pg.121

collective action / collectivity

I often think about Derrick Bell's *Faces at the Bottom of the Well: The Permanence of Racism* (Basic Books, 1992)—the idea of being stuck at the bottom of the well. My friend Rinaldo Anderson was talking about how, the way you get out of the well is to actually stand on each other's shoulders to get out.
Lecture, John Jennings

pg.50

I'm most interested in speculative design's capacity to enable and advance community organizing work. In that endeavor, I think design needs to take a backseat to organizing and the relational work that makes organizing possible.

...

pg.59

With Making Room for Abolition, my underlying, long-term intention was to begin

18

considering what it would take to use futuring as an organizing tool toward abolishing police and prisons.
Interview, Lauren Williams

Where can we locate the revolutionary potential in printing? I think that the first point to take away from this is the importance of collectivity—outside of the confines of wage, labor, and profit, even beyond that which is self-sustaining, or trying to build revolutionary mood.
Lecture, Danielle Aubert

But I think organizing has worked its way into my teaching more around the idea of self-determination. Encouraging students to define what they want, force change, and not wait to be "given" power.
Interview, Danielle Aubert

It is important to recognize these are community-based activities—these forms of action require building solidarity across groups of people and learning how to trust and rely on one another.
Essay, Uzma Z. Rizvi

If Web 1.0 was the laboratory of the one who makes, Web 2.0 is the piazza of the one who speaks. For Arendt, speaking is what leads to action. It is praxis. However, on social media platforms, we mostly get speech without action. Tweeting is like giving an oration in the dark: one doesn't know exactly who is out there, and it may be that nobody is listening.
Interview, Silvio Lorusso

affective connection

I often think about Derrick Bell's Faces at the Bottom of the Well: The Permanence of Racism (Basic Books, 1992)—the idea of being stuck at the bottom of the well. My friend Rinaldo Anderson was talking about how, the way you get out of the well is to actually stand on each other's shoulders to get out.
Lecture, John Jennings

He argued that these kinds of very specific personal stories were more impactful than certain texts on the Marxist theory of value. It can make you really mad and motivated to take action when you read about an injustice happening to somebody else in a situation that is similar to yours. It makes your situation less alienating and it also helps make you feel like you're part of this class of people, together with them.
Lecture, Danielle Aubert

structure (of collectivity)

It isn't really possible to do if there is no center. The center can even be two people working side by side. But "doing the work" is what builds community, what builds relationships, and what, potentially, flattens out relationships.
Interview, Danielle Aubert

horizontal

The Riso became this community where students could come and help each other print and create a lot of work.
Lecture, Elaine Lopez

The practice of decolonial design education is to be found in the ability of managers, coordinators, teachers, and students to position and question their power inside the educational institutions: [...] in creating a horizontal learning dynamic where knowledge is expanded rather than transferred.
Essay, Maya Ober and Hayfaa Chalabi

In it they say that design has gone viral, but it's a dangerous kind of success; it's a success in which design becomes, in a way, more successful than designers.
Lecture, Silvio Lorusso   pg.129

It means asking what role designers play, concretely, in shaping technologies, whether apps or institutions, but also what their actual place in the social structure of organizations is.
...   pg.135
How much agency does a product designer, say, at Amazon actually possess? Does this agency manifest within their design activity, that is, within the products they design, or outside of it, for instance through demands related to working conditions?
...   pg.135
Most activist design faces the same problem: it is stuck in the humanistic, declarative register of outrage. Its job is to assert what's wrong and give form to such assertions. When internet users do more or less the same thing that activist designers do, for instance, by posting a black square on their Instagram profiles, we become aware of the dilution of design into communication at large.
Interview, Silvio Lorusso   pg.136

of educator
In so far as one might claim to be scyborg, that is, s+cyborg—la paperson's queer turn of the word "to name the structural agency of persons who have picked up colonial technologies and reassembled them for decolonizing purposes"—one is, in some measure, always in the process of an undoing and reassembling (xiv).
Essay, Uzma Z. Rizvi   pg.118

cathartic / healing
So I came with this term, the "EthnoGothic," which is about using horror and the technologies of horror to unpack these types of trauma so we can get to a better future.
...   pg.43
I did this visual essay about it, looking at the different ways that horror and dark fantasy and the monstrous actually become cathartic.
Lecture, John Jennings   pg.43

care work
As a female Iraqi Swedish immigrant living in Holland and a female Ashkenazi Jewish immigrant based in Switzerland, we try to support these alienated students with care and compassion, drawing on our own lived experiences of exclusion and discrimination. However, we often fail. The work this entails comes to us as a burden, but it is necessary to take up. Or, perhaps it is a necessary burden. In any case, we are situated at an impasse, which has generated a commitment that also prompts us to ask ourselves if it is futile.
Essay, Maya Ober and Hayfaa Chalabi   pg.107

This is not done in the service of creating new hierarchies, but rather, with a consideration of how care, consent, and a lack of harm may, in fact, be a generative, rather than an extractive form of teaching and learning.
Essay, Uzma Z. Rizvi   pg.121

see labor (pg. 29); see (intentional) slowness (pg. 15??); see many other centers and peripheries (pg. 30); see radical joy (pg. 22); see pedagogy of chaos (pg. 14); see pedagogy of forgiveness (pg. 15); see mechanisms of maintenance (pg. 10)

aesthetic...
of deviation from mainstream aesthetic
In this sense, I believe that nostalgia for the vernacular internet and the apology for online "brutalism" are not coincidental.
Interview, Silvio Lorusso   **21**

craft

Our teachers did encourage in us, sometimes in even crisper Urdu, a love of local art, craft, and tradition.
  Essay, Ahmed Ansari   pg.68

I think it also means leaning into your craft. Your skills and your machines and your workspaces. And being ready to make them available when and if the time comes that people want to use them.
  Lecture, Danielle Aubert   pg.86

So, I guess craft is not exclusively connected to manual production, like the act of printing. It seems to me that one can engage with craft in various ways—it just means knowing your material. I once heard a union organizer say to another union organizer that they admired that person's craft.
  Interview, Danielle Aubert   pg.91

Design is traditionally linked to a division of labor that separates the planner from the maker, the one who manages from the one who executes. In this sense, design is the professionalization of planning. In theory, once this happens there is no craft anymore because both the planner and the executor are alienated from their work—the former stuck in the merely abstract, the latter in the merely concrete.

  But things aren't so symmetrical. An executor has little escape from alienation. The planner, on the other hand, has several chances to work as a craftsperson[...] The figure of the creative coder is another contemporary manifestation of the craftsperson.
  ...   pg.137

Here, we reach an almost paradoxical conclusion: the more designers are professionalized, that is, legitimized as professionals, the more they can be craftspeople.
  ...   pg.137

The web became mainstream through users who acted like craftspeople: they designed and fabricated their personal webpages in relative isolation (a fundamental necessity for the homo faber, according to Arendt). With the advent of the blogosphere, Web 2.0, and later, social media like Facebook, poietic activity—making—became peripheral: from now on, only designers and programmers would craft webpages.
  ...   pg.139

Much design work is political in this very narrow sense—it is declarative, expressive. The activist poster is akin to the political post. Rooting design in craft means going beyond the bold statement, the declaration, the manifesto.
  Interview, Silvio Lorusso   pg.140

see joy (pg. 22)

material condition...

I hope by now it is clear that coloniality, the contours of which are here investigated through the concepts of authenticity and hybridity, nationalism and cosmopolitanism, is much more complex than simple reductions to "South-North," "East-West," "Occident-Orient," "White-Brown" binaries, and that it is also not just an epistemological phenomenon, but very much a material and praxical one: epistemological dimensions cannot be discussed without reference to material ones.
  Essay, Ahmed Ansari   pg.75

How does it disseminate? At what point does the gap between intentions and possible actions become too wide? These considerations are valuable because they might lead to an "object-oriented" idea of ethics. Here, artifacts such as products, services, and organizations have

23

politics that manifest in an operational manner, that is, in the way they work. This is why they're hardly even perceivable as politics. In this context, the designer's intentions are not what matters most, especially when those intentions are declared rather than implemented through decision making. Here's an ethical question: how do words become things?
Interview, Silvio Lorusso

pg.136

of Black Rage

[...] interest in materiality and the form of things that are typically intangible, like rage. I'm interested in how design can push on these questions in ways that traditional research methods like writing, secondary research, or qualitative methods just can't quite get at.

...

pg.35

So I'm thinking about these like physical, tangible vessels into which I place rage. What does the material of rage look like? Is it liquid? Can it transfer it to other things? If I break a vessel that's filled with rage, for example, what if I reconstitute that vessel into something else?
Lecture, Lauren Williams

pg.38

A part of me wonders, though, if what I created actually made Black rage any more legible to anyone other than me—or if it was just another cryptic expression of a feeling that I struggle to articulate even though it is integral and ever-present in all my work and much of my life. I'm also cognizant that, at the end of the day, white people are busy making up their own narratives around Black rage—and countless other "illegible" things about Black experiences and aliveness and death—so, why not shape the narrative with my own contribution?
Interview, Lauren Williams

pg.54

These types of stories were shared precisely to enrage the other workers who might be in another part of the factory and not know that that was going on. There are a lot of these newsletters.
Lecture, Danielle Aubert

pg.84

see reassembling (pg. 25)

of representation and erasure

Critical Race Design Studies is something I came up with. I think about it as an interdisciplinary design practice that intersects critical race theory, speculative design, design history, and critical making to analyze and critique the effects of visual communication, graphic objects, and their associated systemic mediations on racial identity.

...

pg.40

So it was a formal representation of the systems of oppression as design which I found repugnant, but also extremely fascinating to study—the underlying theories and design-oriented rationales for racial oppression, and how to disrupt and retire them from use.

...

pg.40

I started looking at sale papers for slaves—how beautiful, in some ways, they are as objects and how terrifying and how disruptive they were to the people being sold or being turned into objects. That's one of the things that attracts me so much to Afrofuturism, because in a certain sense, you talk about beings who—with a similar document—turned immediately from an object into a person. That's the Emancipation Proclamation, where you shift immediately from being a thing much like a bale of hay or a mule or a horse to an actual person.
Lecture, John Jennings

pg.41

I would posit instead that they may be creating around race in order to make sense of their everyday racialized reality, or to see more work that connects to them because we deserve to be represented in the ways we want to be seen.

...

pg.57

Threading

Does that designer creating work around their race make some quality of their identity more consumable, palatable, or profitable for the machine of racial capitalism or neoliberalism in the process? Are they (inadvertently or not) using the tools of a racist patriarchy to prop up that racist patriarchy?

Initially, I was disappointed by the lack of Black representation in the collection as I moved through the museum; I could not "see" myself among the various European paintings.

The promotional materials in their collections showcased the shifts from stereotypical depictions of Black performers to imagery that aspired to be more authentic in its portrayals.

These racial identifiers appear in graphic design artifacts (as type choice, image style, AAVE vernacular) and reflect the ways in which Black people have been pigeonholed, or, conversely, began to assert greater authority over how they chose to be identified.

This reflexive process is important in today's landscape because it helps build social consciousness and awareness of the impact of representation.

The starter pack foregrounds what is unseen to the insider because it is mundane. For the outsider, unsurprisingly, the medium becomes the message. The starter pack meme highlights something else as well, namely, the fact that identity formation combines work and consumption.

of (design) chaos

Chaos has something to offer: uniqueness. Paraphrasing Tolstoy, whereas projects are all alike, every chaos is messy in its own way. So, what does the chaos at the periphery of design look like? To me, it appears more or less like this: a draconian series of InDesign paragraph styles, a lost Indexhibit site, a logo commissioned ironically on Fiverr, the new MoMA show curated by Paola Antonelli, a heart on an Instagram story by Bráulio Amado, a visit to the final thesis show at the Dutch Academy Eindhoven, a 404 error on a wrong jQuery URL on a static webpage, a bunch of riso-printed zines...

reassembling

I'm working on a horror story and thinking about these things called laughing barrels. Basically, during slavery time, even Black people's joy and laughter were controlled. There were these barrels that you would stick your head in and laugh into. I think that's where they get "a barrel of laughs" from. So, I had this idea that this particular barrel was magical in some way. And then these archeologists find it many, many years later and what's happened is all the laughter that's inside it has fermented...it becomes something else. When it's let out, it becomes this thing called the Side Splitter, and it basically is weaponized as Black laughter.

Departing from Sharpe's In the Wake, Black redactions and annotations reveal new ways of seeing the systems made visible in these images and the violences those systems enact. Further, this work examines the absurdity of what emerges from the wake when calls to redress systems that deliver anti-Black terror are met with empty, performative remedies.

Such experiments create disturbances, open wounds, and produce wakes in these represent-ations of Black people in distress by cutting away at images; recomposing them; trans-forming them into new, abstract, dimensional objects; viewing them through the lens of critical texts; and treating those texts as both material and frame.

...   pg.56

Or, when a designer makes work around race because they want to reclaim some part of themselves they've been compelled to withhold, that feels like a worthy reclaiming of a "master's tool."

Interview, Lauren Williams   pg.57

I liken my process to that of musical sampling because, in many ways, the idea of freestyling and remixing feels like a radical act. One definition of radical can be defined as being, "of or going to the root or origin; fundamental." For me, working with the "root" is key to understanding.

Essay, Kelly Walters   pg.102

As la paperson has identified us, "these subversive beings wreck, scavenge, retool, and reassemble the colonizing university into decolonizing contraptions. They are scyborgs with a decolonizing desire."

Essay, Uzma Z. Rizvi   pg.118

see material condition of (pg. 23)

design, design profession

I'm most interested in using design to do other things that fail to deliver on its capacity to serve capital: to question the political geography of Detroit, to uncover and recover parts of ourselves, to critique oppression.

Interview, Lauren Williams   pg.53

professionalization of design

And then in 1986 the International Typographical Union, which was one of the longest continuously running unions representing typesetters, was dissolved, absorbed into other unions. So the work of typesetters would be done by this emergent and growing category of labor, the graphic designer.

Lecture, Danielle Aubert   pg.85

We can say that design professionalization followed two routes. Let's borrow from Max Weber to identify these routes. First, design grounded its professional authority in rationality—think of the designer as a "scientific" problem solver (in the 1950s advertisers attempted the same). Second, design tried to legitimize itself through charisma—think of the allure of the designer as author, the lifestyle recommendations of Stefan Sagmeister, the cult of Philippe Starck, etc.

...   pg.133

Nowadays, the trendy term that you find in most paper, abstracts, and design events descriptions—"complexity" —doesn't go very far. Because, after all, complexity is reassuring: it suggests that there are experts who can make complexity readable, understandable, and thus simple. That mess can be tamed.

Interview, Silvio Lorusso   pg.141

responsibilization of design

If we ever stopped to take stark account of the brutality of everyday reality in the struggles of those at its vanguard for the things that matter most—not typography or interfaces or service touchpoints, but land, world, labor, freedom—things might sober up in the field and this affective circus of false celebration might give way to harder commitments.

Lecture, Ahmed Ansari   pg.75

How are aesthetic values affected when designers are asked to take on additional responsibilities (such as dismantling structures of capital and responding to climate change)?
Interview, Danielle Aubert and Elaine Lopez

On the left, you see the theoretical self-aggrandizing and self-empowering view of designers [designers can take hold of, dismantle, and rewire some of the abusive structures of capital by manipulating an interplay of physical contours that are also expressing limits, capacities, and values), and then on the right, the most concrete daily reality.
...
This feels a bit out of place, a bit out of proportion. I think that this is a form of field aggrandizement by over-responsibilization. In his book, Monteiro's demonstration is unable to provide any example of a good-doing or evil-doing that is enacted by someone who defines themselves within the design [field]. For example, the main evildoer is an engineer for Volkswagen. Those are the examples he brings in. There isn't even a negative way to demonstrate that power, so this power is probably lacking.
Lecture, Silvio Lorusso

How much agency does a product designer, say, at Amazon actually possess? Does this agency manifest within their design activity, that is, within the products they design, or outside of it, for instance through demands related to working conditions? The problem I see with the "responsible" or "ethical" approach to design is that it is rarely focused on design itself.
...
How does a designer behave ethically or responsibly as a designer, and not as a generic citizen or netizen?
Interview, Silvio Lorusso

design problem-solving
[Question from audience] "Lauren you've mentioned how design is broadly understood as a problem-solving practice. And this notion is being reinforced by design education in a way that is often uncritical and apolitical. I'm interested in how you counter this notion in your teaching and what theories, philosophies, pedagogies, etc., inform your educational practice."
...
But my issue with design being framed in that way is that the way design resolves things is usually cosmetic.
Lecture, Lauren Williams

A lot of speculative design is deeply techno-solutionist at a time when it's more apparent than ever that technology can't save us from ourselves.
Interview, Lauren Williams

Imposing a meaningful order begins with drawing the line that separates what is subject to the design effort from what is not: the former is what designers generally call the "problem." Design is a magic circle that produces an orderly inside and a chaotic outside, safeguarding and reworking the shifting border between the two, and finally placing things and people in one or the other.
Lecture, Silvio Lorusso

design thinking, popularization of design thinking
Before I entered the design field, I had been doing policy, research, and program management targeted at helping low-income families build wealth and economic security. In this role, I was swept up in the wave of design thinking's popularization and became enamored by the promise of what I thought design thinking could offer the nonprofit industrial complex and all its paternalistic baggage: a chance—I hoped—to listen intently to

the audiences we were designing policy and programs for and invite them in as co-designers of "solutions" to address the impediments preventing them from achieving the economic mobility they'd been promised.

...
pg.52

Along the way, thankfully, I was disabused of the naïve hope I initially (mis)placed in design thinking to shift centuries-long patterns of disinvestment, theft, and exploitation by churning out quippy "solutions." I did, however, come to understand that design—broadly interpreted as manipulating materials, forms, and spaces to shape an experience—paired with a critical orientation and a deeper political foundation, could also offer a set of tools for asking crucial questions about why social fictions like racism prevail, why capitalism is so hard to change, and why we continue to distribute power so unevenly. Beyond that, I came to understand it as a tool for "imagining otherwise," to borrow from Christina Sharpe.

Interview, Lauren Williams
pg.53

Design Thinking has been extremely successful at bringing design outside of the design sphere, but at the same time, it has led to a situation in which Design Thinking—the methodology for thinking of problems as design problems—becomes assimilated to other disciplinary fields. The case in point is the fact that business students now study Design Thinking as part of their program. Design Thinking is not necessarily produced by designers themselves, so it's diluted in the sense that it is so successful that it relegates the designer to the side. That's the brilliance of it.

Lecture, Silvio Lorusso
pg.128

---

see threshold (pg. 29)

profitability of design

[...]why US scholars need to engage with the work of global others, particularly when the imperative in the field is to instrumentalize, to convert into use-value, the knowledge systems and perspectives of the latter. Given that the modern academy and institutions like universities and conservatories are themselves entirely compromised spaces that exist to interpellate other knowledges and translate them into palatable and sanitized knowledge-capital[...], perhaps it might be better to leave other knowledges alone.

Essay, Ahmed Ansari
pg.71

Does that designer creating work around their race make some quality of their identity more consumable, palatable, or profitable for the machine of racial capitalism or neoliberalism in the process? Are they (inadvertently or not) using the tools of a racist patriarchy to prop up that racist patriarchy?

Interview, Lauren Williams
pg.57

So from mass production to cultural production, the shift maintains the same mechanism of broadcasting culture, as if culture was an item to be sold to a certain public. We still think of cultural production, to a certain extent, as a form of mass production, while of course the interpretation, the way in which culture is produced, is way more interactive and consumerist.

Lecture, Silvio Lorusso
pg.129

---

disillusion of design

You can say that there is a kind of bonding mechanism to show disillusionment with respect to design and, specifically, graphic design. Design-hating is, to a certain extent and in certain circles, becoming a way to create a sort of belonging.

...
pg.127

The general slogan is this: "With great power comes responsibility." (You know the uncle of Spiderman, who is often quoted in design presentations?) At the same time, there is a

reality check made of lack of recognition, and so on and so forth. I think it's through this very mechanism that a sense of disillusionment and trauma, professional trauma, comes to the fore.
Lecture, Silvio Lorusso   pg.131

threshold...
of technical / of design

I often get asked what epistemic decolonisation might lead to in terms of a new design praxis. My answer to this is that at its heart, the project of decentering US- and EU-centric conceptions of design has to start with opening up the question of what design is.
Essay, Ahmed Ansari   pg.74

So the budget holder becomes the designer, anybody who has a certain influence on it becomes the designer. The larger scope of this argument was made by the art historian Victor Margolin. And of course, you cannot deny that what he says is true—the fact that we as humans are designing species. But there is a big gap between this idea that "humans design" and the specific culture of industrial design that, nowadays, we just call "design." This is something that Papanek was bringing to the table, that in the beginning, there was design but not industrial design. There is a mismatch in understanding. It's like, we think that this generic human activity has the same logic, the same principle, the same philosophy as something that was born a century ago.
Lecture, Silvio Lorusso   pg.130

Designers are attempting to gain cultural authority. This differs slightly from the blend of the rational and the charismatic I just described. Cultural authority turns the technical into the humanistic.
...   pg.134

It shows how the threshold of what we refer to as the "technical" shifts. Writing an email in the '90s meant you were a tech-savvy person, an expert; today it means you're just an average computer user. The technicity of such practice has faded into the background. What technicities have dissolved in design? Which ones need to be foregrounded again?
...   pg.134

The web became mainstream through users who acted like craftspeople: they designed and fabricated their personal webpages in relative isolation (a fundamental necessity for the homo faber, according to Arendt). With the advent of the blogosphere, Web 2.0, and later, social media like Facebook, poietic activity—making—became peripheral: from now on, only designers and programmers would craft webpages.
Interview, Silvio Lorusso   pg.139

of "problem"

In general, what I'm trying to point out is the fragile threshold of what we call a "project"— the "definition of a design problem"—and the fact that there is a growing realization that this threshold is consensual and ritualistic to a certain extent, that there is something esoteric about it. I guess this gives you a bit of an idea of the diagnosis.
        In the fragility of this consensus is the creation of an inside and an outside. There is a growing sense of disillusionment.
Lecture, Silvio Lorusso   pg.127

labor

We seem to place undue pressure on racialized designers to do the work of undoing racism, when what they need or desire, instead, might be the freedom to make the work that feels truest to them.
Interview, Lauren Williams   pg.57

It is my observation, and again, this perhaps invites challenging, that the burden of labor in providing non-US accounts of design largely falls on immigrant designers, design educators, and students. This reliance on immigrant accounts is also not without its problems, for it glosses over the issue of the reliability of immigrant interlocution: it assumes that immigrant scholars and students have "done their homework" in critically thinking through their own subject-positions and being careful about their translations of their root cultures.

Essay, Ahmed Ansari pg.71

So the work of typesetters would be done by this emergent and growing category of labor, the graphic designer.

Lecture, Danielle Aubert pg.85

When predominantly white, hetero-patriarchal institutions are challenged to "decolonize," it is often marginalized students who are burdened with providing solutions to design schools and the oppressive legacy of design in curricula.

... pg.107

The onus for transforming design education and practice towards a more critical and equitable one lies on the shoulders of student-led initiatives or activist teachers.

... pg.107

Instead of accountability toward violent educational systems that privilege certain voices over others, these institutions decide to put the labor of deconstructing oppressive histories on the systemically marginalized.

Essay, Maya Ober and Hayfaa Chalabi pg.108

Service is directly related to labor outside the classroom that a faculty or teaching staff does to support the academic frameworks, policies, procedures, and systems established in the institution of higher education.

... pg.118

Understanding service as decolonizing, justice work for our students and the institute may explain why research shows that women and BIPOC scholars end up doing so much more service as care work for institutions.

Essay, Uzma Z. Rizvi pg.119

see cathartic / healing (pg. 21)

capitalism
see craft (pg. 23); see joy (pg. 22); see profitability of design (pg. 28)

many other centers and peripheries
Clearly, Pakistani bureaucrats and educators seem to view their societies in much the same way their American and European interlocutors have: not, as the Sri Lankan anthropologist Gananath Obeyesekere argued in his famous 1992 debate with Marshall Sahlins (Obeyesekere, 1992; Sahlins, 1995), as equal torchbearers of the values the European Enlightenment claimed to exemplify, but as absolutely, incommensurately different from the West, and their absolute alterity must be respected and maintained.

Essay, Ahmed Ansari pg.66

For anyone who has taught in the Academy, we know that the replication of violence is embedded in the structures of teaching, for example, the ways by which we insist that our students replicate, cite, and know the classics, the core, the foundations.

... pg.120

"We must recognize that for our students, the lifting and celebration of a particular form of knowledge is often at the expense, erasure, and replacement of their life experiences and histories."

Essay, Uzma Z. Rizvi pg.120

30

inbetweener

Despite so many years of traveling back and forth between Pakistan and the United States, I have never been able to make up my mind about whether Pakistani design education is too closeted and provincial, too used to engaging with its own issues within its own narrow sense of the immediate world and the horizon of its historical and institutional affinities, or whether it is global in the truest sense of the word, often incorporating and transmuting ideas, practices, and tools from outside into recognisable but nevertheless new forms.

...   pg.67

There is no doubt in my mind that what the school represented was something as local as it was foreign, as much shaped by the city and country and its influences as it was by colonial ones. [...] Perhaps a better way of framing the work that the students produce in Pakistan is that it is something hybrid, engaging with and speaking of a world to which they do-but-not-quite belong in their largely English-educated, middle-class sensibilities, which nevertheless deals with everyday reality in Karachi and understands and interprets it in ways that no foreign tourist or Western academic could.

Essay, Ahmed Ansari   pg.68

There is a very fine line many of us walk; one only has to think back to Franz Fanon's Black Skin, White Masks (1952) and how the deep colonization of the self comes to the fore to be confronted with the complexity of what being a scyborg might really mean. What are we trying to undo when we ourselves are defined by this system of oppression masked as a hub of knowledge?

...   pg.118

This text is, as Marcelo Diversi and Claudio Moreira write, the work of a betweener, the "(un)conscious bodies experiencing life in and between two cultures" (Diversi and Moreira 2009, 19). In fact, it is often the betweener who finds themselves pulling together our realities on the scraps of colonial technologies, as we embody a code-switching scyborg to retool, reframe, rework, and transform our collective futures.

Essay, Uzma Z. Rizvi   pg.119

The term double bind comes from anthropologist Gregory Bateson, and it refers to the idea that you get a signal from society or from a person, and at the same time, at the same level, you get a conflicting one.

...   pg.130

On the left, you see the theoretical self-aggrandizing and self-empowering view of designers [designers can take hold of, dismantle, and rewire some of the abusive structures of capital by manipulating an interplay of physical contours that are also expressing limits, capacities, and values), and then on the right, the most concrete daily reality .

Lecture, Silvio Lorusso   pg.131

Critiquing

Design, Race, and Speculation:
From Horror to the Specter of Black Liberation
A Conversation Between Lauren Williams and John Jennings

Join Lauren Williams and John Jennings in a conversation that explores
their respective practices through the speculative dimensions of design, race,
and time. The entanglement of these topics in the presenters' practices is
both banal and charged with rage and monstrous horror.

Yet one sees their work, each in its own way, as responding to Walidah
Imarisha's assertion that "all organizing is science fiction... moving beyond
the boundaries of what is possible or realistic, into the realm of what we
are told is impossible." What does a liberated Black future look like? What
is it made of? How does it come to be?

LAUREN WILLIAMS

Race as Technology

I'll start by sharing a little bit
of framing about the three themes
that you see on these slides:
time, design, and racism. Then,
I'll try to walk through a few
of my own projects. Two of which,
admittedly, are in pretty early
development. They won't be demonstrations of work, but more like
talking through what I'm working
on. I'm also looking forward to
questions people have, or insights
that might inform the directions
I'm going in with this work.

It's important to state
that most of my work rests on
an understanding that race is
something that has been designed.
And by that, I mean, it has
been deliberately crafted and
imbued with a set of functions
and features, most of which I
would argue concern its capacity to keep people organized
and oppressed in the ways that
capitalism requires to extract
and hoard wealth. So, most of my
work emerges from a recognition
of this idea and a desire to
make people understand that this
is a deliberate, intentionally
produced technology of sorts.
I think John [Jennings] will
probably talk a little bit about
how he sees racist technology
too, later.

projection →

speculation
of social
fictions →

← (myth of)
neutrality

Another thing that I think
kind of falls into this category
is something John said when we
first met, which was that race is
the ultimate "diegetic prototype."
I was like, that's it—that's
what I want to say. I think that
really sums up how I see race
functioning. When I say diegetic
prototype, what I mean is an
object or experience, usually a
technological one, that lives in
a fictional world. Diegesis is
a term that comes from film. I
find myself often working through
producing diegetic prototypes
as a way to ask the questions
I'm exploring in my research or
to push on these definitions of
race as something that is real.

So, when I work through
design, I'm often making diegetic
prototypes that question the
construct of race, or bend
our conception of time in some
way, like proposing a different
kind of future, or a different
understanding of race or racism.
For me, design is only one way ← structural
that I arrive at these questions   agency of
about how oppression works   designer
and why, and what can be done
about it. As I mentioned in the
beginning, I also organize; I've
done policy work and qualitative
research in the past, all around
similar themes such as economic
oppression and inequality. But
now that I know how to design
stuff, I like to throw that into
the mix as well.

collective action/
collectivity →

material
condition of →

projection →

time →

Another thread of design that you'll see in the last project I'll share today is interest in materiality and the form of things that are typically intangible, like rage. I'm interested in how design can push on these questions in ways that traditional research methods like writing, secondary research, or qualitative methods just can't quite get at.

When I think about racism, it's significant to me because of who I am—I'm Black—and more broadly, I'm interested in the ways we organize ourselves, in how we treat each other, and how power distorts our perceptions of each other. I also feel like because racism is something that's been designed—and I see it as either a designed object, an artifact, or a technology—design lends a particularly interesting set of tools to investigate racism. Because we can work with form, we can work with materiality, and we can construct these prototypes that I mentioned in the beginning. We can challenge or unsettle the notion of race as something real in the world.

Lastly, I think about time in my work and it comes up in a couple of ways. In a sense, when I'm talking about racism or working through projects where racism is the question, I'm often thinking about histories that are inherited. But then, at the same time, a lot of my work is looking at how we produce futures without racism, for example, how we draw that future closer together with our present reality and with those histories we've inherited.

Tribute: Tool for
Participating Civically

The first project, I will show you features someone who's actually on the call today. This is some of my thesis work from my MFA program. *Tribute* is a collection of fictional objects from a future world that forces us to rethink how policymaking happens and how civic engagement functions today. In this world, every American resident has a device that functions a little bit like a Tamagotchi, which is a pet alien toy that many of us might remember from the '80s and '90s. The device is a tool for participating civically as a member of American society. The twist here is that unlike caring for a Tamagotchi, cleaning up its poop and feeding it and playing with it, and all that, with this device who you're caring for is your local council person. So, if you neglect your civic duties, if you neglect to vote, if you neglect to pay your taxes, fill out the census, etc., the physiological wellbeing of that councilperson suffers.

The point was not to propose this as a solution to shitty government, although I might be at that point today. Instead, it was meant to embody a critique that I held about power and policymaking and how we engage civically in the world, and about the misuse of power that I interpreted, at least at the time, in how a lot of policymakers in the United States at various levels—state, federal, municipal—disregard the needs and livelihoods of their constituents in the interest of something else, usually themselves or money.

In terms of time, this project was looking at this dystopic future world. In terms of race or racism, I was thinking about how policymaking disregards or devalues certain lives based on race. And then in terms of design, this project relied very heavily on a diegetic prototype.

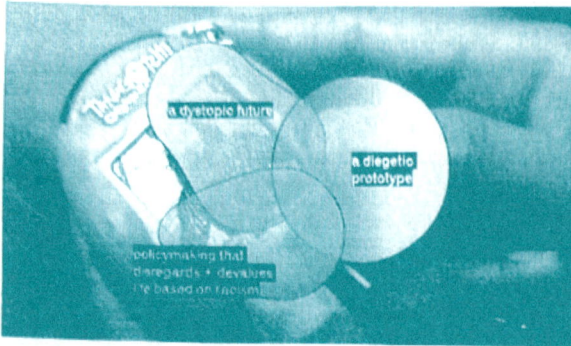

Lauren Williams, lecture slide. Oct 2020.

So, I made the device itself. It worked in the sense that you could pretend to control your policymaker. It was really important to enact it. So, I put it into these scenes in which I would invite people to pretend that they were from this future, pretend that they were a blogger, and then act out an entire blogger scene in which they review the product. And part of this, for me was about how I, as a researcher at the time, was thinking about how to ask these questions about power I have without just sitting down and asking someone outright. How do I get them to embody the idea that they inhabit this future world? So what you're seeing is one example of these blogging scenarios.

The person in our call who took part in the project is someone who actually works in city government in Los Angeles, obviously is Black, and had a lot of reflections about trust and perception of the project within his inner circle. How would his grandmother feel about it? He was like, *she would never trust this thing*. He wonders in the beginning if it has a microphone in it. So, in this way, I was kind of getting at these questions about trust and power

and our political beliefs without just being like, *What do you think about power?* So, that is how I tried to use a diegetic prototype in this scenario.

We were also talking a bit today about horror and I think, in a sense, this device presents a horrific scenario, which is that you could theoretically kill your policymaker by not doing your civic duties. At the same time though, it's also very much bringing up the horrors of daily life that people already experience. So in this case, KP [a participant] was reflecting a lot about surveillance, and these things that are very much real horrors in a lot of Black people's lives today.

Artifacts from a Liberated Detroit

The next project I'll talk about is one that I have not done yet. But I'm really excited about it. I'm working on it right now. It's a project called *Artifacts from a Liberated Detroit*.

What I'm proposing, similar to the last project, is essentially creating a room from an apartment or a house from a future in which we do not have police or incarceration. My plan is to build a room filled with things that are ubiquitous, things that you would typically see in a home, things that would point to the realities that are fundamentally different about a world in which abolition has become a reality. I'm asking these questions: What is life without policing? Without incarceration? I live on a block where cops often run up and down the street to hit their monthly quota for tickets. So, a lot of times I hear sirens. A lot of times, I see the flashing of [emergency] lights reflecting in my apartment before I even hear the siren. I'm thinking about things as mundane as the soundtrack of the

36

neighborhood. If we don't hear sirens, if we don't see lights disrupting the landscape, what would fill in that place?

So, in this case, I'm thinking about a future that I perceive as utopic. I recognize that's not the case for everybody. I'm thinking about design again in the sense that I'm looking at how to produce diegetic prototypes and build a world to help someone imagine and really grasp the urgency and possibility of abolition. When I think about race in this case, I'm thinking a lot about the present-day racism we see manifested in policing and incarceration.

I had a conversation the other day with a friend in which we asked: What if sunflowers, instead of turning toward the sun, turn because of conflict? What if they react to their social environments, for example, as much as, or instead of, the natural environment? What would that mean? What are the implications? For this abolitionist world, I'm thinking about questions like: What would the skyline look like? What if GM—the iconic tower in Detroit that can be seen down Woodward—were owned by someone else? What, for example, are the addresses mail is addressed to? If I'm looking at a table with a pile of old letters on it, are they addressed to me in Detroit or are they addressed to Waawiyaatanong, which is the Indigenous territory we occupy? I'm also thinking about things like, in an abolitionist world, would I even have a water bill? Detroit is notorious for having shut off—and continuing to shut off in the middle of a pandemic— Black people's water access in their homes. And so instead of seeing a water bill strewn on a table, what would be there in its place? What artifacts would take its place? I was on a call earlier this week about my neighborhood, and the neighborhood police officer was explaining her role. And I was like, what if instead of a roving neighborhood police officer, we had something else roving, a roving mental health provide…anything but that. So, these are some of the questions I'm asking. Whose home is it? And what are the artifacts of their daily life and their labor? Is there a uniform in the closet? What kind of uniform is it? What kind of work might they do in this future?

Both projects I just talked about are in essence design fictions that rely on these diegetic prototypes, but they serve completely different purposes. So, for example, in *Tribute*, I was using these objects and the ways I tried to enact them to levy a critique about today. With *Artifacts from a Liberated Detroit*, I'm thinking more about how I can use these objects to suspend people's disbelief about the possibility and urgency of abolition. In both cases, an important part of what I'm trying to do is use visuals and narrative, in some cases experience and experiential rhetorics, to contextualize these ideas that people today still think are too far off to be believable. That's what I'm trying to invite people into with both of these projects.

Black Rage: Borne of Chronic Waiting

The last project I will talk about is *Black Rage*. This is the cover of a book by two psychiatrists from the '60s. The artwork on the cover is a set of annotations by the artist Glenn Ligon. I'm thinking about Black rage as a product of chronic waiting.

inertia
(waiting) →

Back to the three intersections… In thinking about time here, it comes in a different dimension: I'm thinking about waiting for something that is delayed or waiting for something that's past due. I think about Black rage as a product of repeated racism over time. When ↖ pg.50 I think about design in this case, I think it looks a little bit more like art, if people are strict about their distinctions between the two. I'm interested in how meaning is produced and how form reflects some of that meaning.

Lauren Williams, lecture slide. Oct 2020.

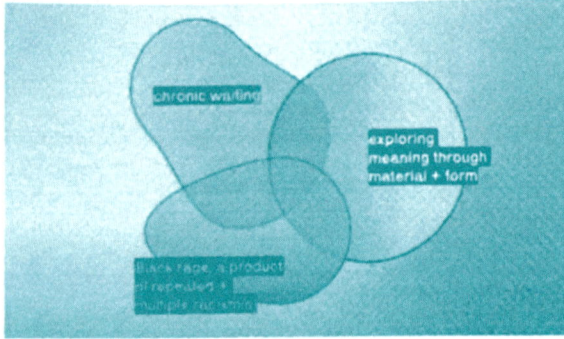

So, when I talk about waiting, with this project I'm thinking about the reality of how long Black people in the US and many other places have been demanding a particular kind of freedom or justice and been told to wait for it. Being told to wait for your life to matter, to echo the demand of Black Lives Matter. I'm not saying that I think Black people have been passively waiting over time to be delivered from injustice, but instead that historically, the trend has been for the nation as a whole to admonish Black people for being patient, for making demands in a particular way that's palat-able and acceptable, and for accepting performative gestures   ← cosmetic change/ empty gestures like the street scale mural that you see in the background here, instead of a response to the demands they're actually asking for. So, when I think of it this way, I'm reminded of this poem by Langston Hughes titled "Harlem," about the material qualities of   material condition of Black rage → this waiting and in this rage. It

↘ affective connection

opens, "What happens to a dream deferred?" And continues:

> Does it dry up
> like a raisin in the sun?
> Or fester like a sore—
> And then run?
> Does it stink like rotten meat?
> Or crust and sugar over—
> like a syrupy sweet?
>
> Maybe it just sags
> like a heavy load.
>
> *Or does it explode?*[1]   Langston Hughes, "Harlem [2]," from *The Collected Works of Langston Hughes*, ed. Arnold Rampersad (Columbia: University of Missouri Press, 2001), 426. Reprinted with permission from Penguin Random House

This is a research project. I have ideas about what I want to make, but I almost don't want to say them because they're changing as I go. These are some sketches I made a couple weeks ago about the things that moti-vate my rage. When I think about these murals that have sprung up over the summer in response to people saying, "stop killing us," "stop policing us in this way," etc., I feel like all these roads, all these murals lead to rage. I'm working through this in sketches, and I think what I really want to get at is these questions: What forms does rage take? How does it get contained? How does it get expressed? And what can it do, what potential does it have?

I think that the chicken wing is here, 'cause in one of my early ideas with this project, I imagined that I would make thousands of vessels. I was playing around with 3D printing ceramics and I was like, *Where do I put my rage normally, where do I place it?* Usually it goes into food, and often it's chicken wings. I've been a vege-tarian for several years except when I am filled with rage, in which case I immediately go and get some wings. So I'm thinking about these like physical, tangi-ble vessels into which I place rage.

What does the material of rage look like? Is it liquid? Can it transfer it to other things? If I break a vessel that's filled with rage, for example, what if I reconstitute that vessel into something else? So, this is really wide open and I'm still working on it, but these are a lot of the questions I'm pursuing.

← re-assembling

↖ pg.96

JOHN JENNINGS

I'm always talking about Afro-futurism. I'll talk about the idea of race as a design object–as a type of deliverable, a type of, I mean, because we talked about it as a system all the time–you know, design as a system of racism as a system. And, you know, logically I'm like, well, I'm a designer, so I want to know what the blueprint looks like, so we can redesign it. Cause we redesigned everything else, you know? So my whole thing is like, well, race must have been working for somebody, never worked for me. We have to figure that out.

projection →
↖ pg. 118

← mechanism
of maintenance

I'm going to start sharing my screen. I'll talk very hastily so we can have more of a conversation. So, this is a talk I didn't get a chance to do over the summer, because of George Floyd murder. I was an advisor for the Sundance Institute, the New Frontier Story Lab, and I was going to talk about this idea, but then the George Floyd incident happened and I just didn't feel like talking about it.

Stereotypes

W.E.B. DuBois, who is very influential for me, was not only a science-fiction writer, but also a sociologist and an information designer.

"The problem of the twentieth century is a problem with the color line," wrote W.E.B. DuBois in 1903.[2] My only thing about this is that he wasn't thinking

far enough into it. I guess he thought that by the twenty-first century, this wouldn't be an issue, but some things like racism are really well designed. That's one of the things I admire about race and stereotypes in general. One of my favorite quotes about race is from Charles W. Mills's the *Racial Contract*, where he posits race as a kind of virtual reality, as a construct itself. This idea of the projection of race onto unwanted people is really interesting:

"There will be white mythologies, invented Orients, invented Africas, invented Americas, with a correspondingly fabricated population, countries that never were, inhabited by people who never were–Calibans and Tontos, Man Fridays and Sambos–but who attain a virtual reality through their existence in travelers' tales, folk myth, popular and highbrow fiction, colonial reports, scholarly theory, Hollywood cinema, living in the white imagination and determinedly imposed on their alarmed real-life counterparts."[3]

I often talk to my students about this notion of the stereotype, which of course comes from design parlance: it's an idea created by Firmin Didot in the 1800s as a printing term. We don't really think about stereotypes the way we talk about them now until like the mid-early 20s; Walter Lipmann, I think, re-appropriated that term and then started using it to talk about pre-judging people. The root word of stereotype is the word *stereos*, which means "hard" or "fixed." It's this fixity that I think people of color, or whoever is being stereotyped, are always trying

3   Charles W. Mills, *The Racial Contract* (Ithaca: Cornell University Press, 1997) 18–10.

2   W.E.B. DuBois, *The Souls of Black Folk* (New York: New American Library, 1903), 10.

to circumvent or escape. This notion of escape is something I think is really important, and I was already thinking about this for a long time.

My background is in graphic design. I've taught design methodology, design history–I've taught courses on what I call "applied semiotics for designers." I taught a course on hip hop and design, another one which I called "Race as Science Fiction," though it was actually an Afrofuturist design studio. Some of these ideas have been forming for a while.

When I was introduced to the idea of speculative design, it was at a critical point when I was really tired of thinking about design. I was thinking about the fact that, most of the time, people we taught graphic design to would go into the world and end up working for the system, end up working for marketing firms, and not really thinking about the ethics of what was happening. This is one of the reasons I ended up teaching in media studies instead of design, because I felt like some art schools are very, very limiting in terms of how they think about these things.

For a long time, I was a fly in the buttermilk, so to speak– I was the third African American person to get an MFA in design from the University of Illinois. I was, I think, the second to get tenure in art there. That was 2009. I mentored the third one, to a certain degree, in 2015. I want to get to a point where there's no more Black firsts, and we can get to that mundane space where people are just hanging out. I don't have to be Black and special at the same time. But I feel like I'm getting off topic.

material condition of →

← design profession

mechanism of maintenance →

material condition of →

unmaintain/ undoing →

Critical Race Design Studies

Critical Race Design Studies is something I came up with. I think about it as an interdisciplinary design practice that intersects critical race theory, speculative design, design history, and critical making to analyze and critique the effects of visual communication, graphic objects, and their associated systemic mediations on racial identity.

I'm designing a course about this right now to analyze, interpret, and critique the formal graphic indexes of racial oppression and our visual culture landscape. I'm from the South, originally from Mississippi. I grew up in post-civil rights Mississippi, where systems of oppression are ubiquitous. You don't really notice them because they're like water. Think about Jim Crow signage, for instance. Jim Crow was a law that said that Black people could not access certain spaces; these spaces had signage up that was designed by municipalities. So I'm thinking, there have to be design specs, there have to be templates for this type of design so that they could all be the same. because that's part of how design works.

So it was a formal representation of the systems of oppression as design which I found repugnant, but also extremely fascinating to study–the underlying theories and design-oriented rationales for racial oppression, and how to disrupt and retire them from use. Again, we redesigned everything else. We're really good at actually updating things. Every time you look around, a new app for your phone is updating itself. So I think we should probably rethink how we think about racial identity. That's all I'm saying.

The other thing is to study how the racially oppressed

appropriate these indexes and theories for liberation and resistance–and this is something that I talk about in my Afrofuturism course. I call these "liberation technologies." It's the idea that the oppressed generally have more of an idea of the system that is oppressing them than the people who are benefiting from it or have created it. This is because, a lot of times, we're trying to get out of it. To borrow from Jordan Peele: we gotta "get out." You have to understand the system so that you can hack it, and that's kind of where we're getting at with these ideas of liberation technologies. Sometimes those technologies are just as mundane as learning how to read and write, for instance, which was why slaves were forbidden to read and write. That particular technology would allow for so much advancement and also for the creation of new designs and narratives that uplifted oppressed bodies and identities to create and disseminate deliverables that critique and expose racial oppression.

When I think about Black designers or designers who are dealing with race, I actually extend my notion of design. I was thinking a lot about people like Carrie Mae Weems, Amos Paul Kennedy Jr.–people who are using text and image like a designer would to talk about race.

The first time I realized I was Black was after I saw *not* the new *Roots*, but the old *Roots*, which came out 1977. It's weird to not know that, and then realize you're Black. But that was the first time I realized, now wait a minute: *I'm Black*. And then: *These people look like my granddaddy and they were owned by white people*. That's a lot to unpack, when you first come to that as a realization. I started thinking about this idea of the

palimpsest, which is a design history term. Basically, it's a piece of parchment that gets reused over and over again. And this part right here is always one of the most disturbing pieces about it. Kunta Kinte is played by the great LeVar Burton–also known as Geordi La Forge–and he's trying to hold onto the name that actually connects him to his culture. And this slave owner, the slave master is saying, "No, your name is Toby." But he won't relent. He was actually like, "I'm not going to give up that name because that's one of the only things that connects me to my home place." So he's literally being rewritten with whip strokes. It's extremely harrowing. Little by little, he slowly becomes Toby. And there's a point where he's both–I call it the "KunToby"– a moment when he's basically cooked the Kente and actually decides that in order for him to survive in this new and strange world, he's going to have to be Toby, but inside he's Kunta Kinte.

That's something that I think about a lot as far as what has to be given up to actually survive. And in terms of the many names that get projected upon the Black body as a palimpsest "Afrikan; cargo; slave; n*****; colored; negro; Afro-American; Black; African American." A lot of those names, we don't choose either. They are projected.

I'm going to go through my favorite quote from Amiri Baraka: "Machines have the morality of their inventors."[4] All different types of technologies take on the ethics of the creators. This is obviously referring to some of the notions I was talking about earlier.

I started looking at sale papers for slaves–how beautiful, in some ways, they are as objects and how terrifying and how disruptive they were to

4   Imamu Amiri Baraka, "Technology & Ethos," in *Raise, Race, Rays, Raze: Essays Since 1965*, ed. Imamu Amiri Baraka (New York, Random House, 1971), 155-57.

material condition of →

the people being sold or being turned *into* objects. That's one of the things that attracts me so much to Afrofuturism, because in a certain sense, you talk about beings who-with a similar document-turned immediately from an object into a person. That's the Emancipation Proclamation, where you shift immediately from being a thing much like a bale of hay or a mule or a horse to an actual person. You cease being a type of soft machine or a type of prosthetic of the master's whim and are now able to utilize technology, which is extremely empowering. Those are some of the things that I'm thinking about with that work. I found this document in a book-a notice that was printed up in New Orleans to stop white kids from listening to this "Negro music,":

Obviously they had not heard of Kendrick Lamar. You know what I'm saying? Anyway, nevermind... "[t]he savage music of these records are undermining the morals of our white youth in America. Call the advertisers in the radio stations that played this type of music and complain to them! Don't Let Your Children Buy, or Listen To These Negro Records."

I forgot when this was printed, but this is the Citizens' Council of Greater New Orleans. Anyway, I'm going to very quickly shift over to this idea about horror.

NOTICE!
STOP

Help Save The Youth of America
DON'T BUY NEGRO RECORDS

(If you don't want to serve negroes in your place of business, then do not have negro records on your juke box or listen to negro records on the radio.)

The screaming, idiotic words, and savage music of these records are undermining the morals of our white youth in America.

Call the advertisers of the radio stations that play this type of music and complain to them!

Don't Let Your Children Buy, or Listen To These Negro Records

For additional copies of this circular, write
CITIZENS' COUNCIL OF GREATER NEW ORLEANS, INC.
509 Delta Building   New Orleans, Louisiana 70112

Permission is granted to re-print this circular

Horror and EthnoGothic

Seeing Black history and stuff I grew up talking about or knowing about on television, like, "Oh my God! The Tulsa race massacre— That was horrible!" Yes, it truly was. And it was so much more. Or, "Oh my God—sundown towns! I never heard of that!" In fact, some of them are still sundown towns.

I was thinking about the idea of Afrofuturism. It seemed to me at a particular point, everything that was Black and speculative was being shoved under Afrofuturism. And I was like, do you ignore genre? I'm a genre fanatic. Look at something like *Kindred*, which is about a Black woman who is drawn inex- plicably back through to slavery time-that's a time travel story, but there's no time machine.

42

There's no TARDIS or DeLorean to draw her back. Some kind of mystical or otherworldly technology does. And then of course there are aspects of that particular narrative that actually map themselves more readily onto the gothic than onto sci-fi. So I came with this term, the "Ethno-Gothic," which is about using horror and the technologies of horror to unpack these types of trauma so we can get to a better future. ← cathartic/ healing

I always use Erica Badu's song "Bag Lady" as a perfect example. If you haven't heard it, shame on you. Go listen to it (they have this thing called Spotify. I'm sure you could find it). You have this bag lady, a homeless woman, who is trying to catch a bus and she's being weighed down by all these bags. And so Erica Badu was like, you need to pack light so you can get on that bus. I imagine that the bus is going to the Afrofuture and that the bag is filled with trauma from slavery; epigenetic trauma; all kinds of evil, horrible things in the bags; monsters. So, the idea is unpacking that so you can go forward. My friend Stanford Carpenter and I came up with this idea of the EthnoGothic and I did this visual essay about it, looking at the different ways that horror and dark fantasy and the monstrous actually become ← cathartic/ healing
cathartic.

And then I started thinking about my upbringing in Mississippi, listening to the blues–people like Robert Johnson, for instance, and his fictitious cousin, a character of mine called Frank Half-dead Johnson. But instead of learning how to become a more talented blues player… Basically, he loses his family to racialized violence and goes to the crossroads to become a better conjure man [Ed. note: An Americanism,

similar meaning to witch doctor] to exact his revenge upon the white landowners who killed his family. And then he's beholden to the Devil, or scratch [Ed. note: Street name for an opioid, i.e., Vicodin.], in this particular sense, and ends up having to basically work off his debt to the devil, so to speak, by acting as his interlocutor and collecting souls that resonate in a particular frequency; he's composing a song with these souls.

The current book I'm working on is called *Box of Bones*. This actually relates to some of the things Lauren was talking about–the idea of waiting, particularly, for freedom, waiting for that dream to be undeferred, so to speak. These covers are by the wonderful Stacy Robinson, who is my friend and partner in Black Kirby–a studio we created when we were at the University at Buffalo. It's a ten-part narrative focused on a Black woman named Lindsay Ford, who is from the South; she comes up with a grandfather who is a Black blues man, who tells her about this box that actually punishes the wicked–people who hurt Black people–but there's always a cost to exact. Some people call it the "box of pain"; some people call it the "black box." Most people call it the "box of bones." So this is a diegetic prototype that deals with the question of where rage goes. Rage manifests itself as these different monsters. Not like Black vampires or Black werewolves, but creatures that were created from Black horrors or Black fears. For instance, this character called The Wretched; it's literally a sentient lynching tree. And the word "wretched" of course comes from Frantz Fanon's *The Wretched of the Earth*, while the baboon character comes from this quote from Toni Morrison's *Beloved* and the little "pic*****nies" hanging from the tree, who are actually former people who are turned into stereotypes and are forced to hang in the tree and serve The Wretched forever.

This next character is The Suffering. The Suffering is designed to be a darker side of how Black masculinity is shown. The Dark is kind of like my Pinhead character. I always called this character an Afro-centric Hell Raiser to a certain degree. He's this minstrelized character that actually runs the rest of these whatnots living inside the box.

The middle character is called The Nobody because it doesn't have a body; it actually references that song "Nobody Knows the Trouble I've Seen" [Ed. note: An African American spiritual song standard] It represents the emptying of Black culture, the form taking over

the content of Black culture and being sold back to us. It's kind of empty inside—and when it jumps on top of your head it can control your body. And once it leaves your body, it takes your head with it and people don't know where the head goes. And then there is this thing is called The Burden; it's essentially a manifestation of slavery. It's a giant cotton sack filled with body parts of slaves, and he crawls around to replenish the body parts.

And there is the Night Doctor, which is a story that was told to slaves to keep them in line. Back in the day that, people were stealing people to do medical experiments on them. So this character represents medical apartheid.

I'm going to stop there because I have a lot more, but I'm very excited to interact with Lauren.

Q & A

Lauren

I think you talked about how we should redesign things like race. We redesign everything else. I've thought about that a lot too. I'm with you, but also, if somebody comes in and tries to do a "Let's redesign race project," I might be, "Oh no...." I don't think that's what you mean, but design loves to solve things. Even the department I teach in, I hear other faculty tell students, "If you're working on a poster project, your poster is the solution." And I'm just like, *It's not...* What is it a solution to? It's just a poster.

I've thought a lot about how race has already been innovated on. Post-raciality, for example, is an innovation on race. The idea that race is no more, that because we've had our Black president, racism can't possibly still exist in this world because the highest possible office has been occupied by a Black person. Ruha Benjamin has written about how this very specific idea of post-raciality is an innovation on race and how the news has been replaced with surveillance technologies that get upgraded over time.

44

In terms of trying to formulate a response to what you shared, I am super interested in talking more about horror. I don't have a coherent thought yet, but I feel like we should go there.

On Horror

John

I've been thinking a lot about horror, because we live in such dark spaces. Not that I'm an Afro-pessimist—the word "pessimism" bothers me. I feel like I can't be a dad, teach, and be pessimistic. Maybe I'm being too literal about that, but I've always been a massive horror fan...

Fairly recently, there has been the show *Lovecraft Country* (2020), which I call "race craft-ian and horror" because it's like.... There's this book called *Racecraft: The Soul of Inequality in American Life* [by Karen E. Fields and Barbara J. Fields published by Verso, 2014] that looks at race as a spell, a type of mystical spell. It's by these two sisters, they're not only Black women, they're actually siblings. H. P. Lovecraft obviously was a raging racist, but he also gave us such interesting tools to talk about metaphor and monstrosity and all these different things. It's very, very interesting.

And his world-building was fantastic. I'm sorry, dude was really talented. The idea of open-source world-building is something I think he really... But he was deeply xenophobic. And there are some folks like Misha Green and others who've been dealing with that.

I teach a course called "Afrofuturism and the Visual Cultures of Horror." We look at stuff like *Tales from the Hood* (1995) and *Candyman* (2021) and all these different films that are coming out. I'm dealing with the useful nature of horror; how horror can comfort us and give us a space in which we can experience these things at a distance.

...

The idea of "passing"–"Chitlin-hacking" is what I call it (because I'm from the South) is taking something that was supposed to destroy you and then actually flipping the script and turning it into something that can feed you, in some way. So people who could pass for white, for instance, used their phenotype and their physicality to look "white" and just became white–thousands of

people. The horror is, though, that you have to
pretend to be someone else for the rest of your
life.

Lauren

I'm thinking also about Black capitalists, for
example, not passing phenotypically, but passing
or acculturating economically, which is really the
primary function of race anyway. That happens all
the time. I'm not sure how many people on this
call have seen Lil Wayne's latest announcement.
But I think moments like that with celebrities...
I don't want to get into it, but I feel like
they're to the question of, "Can race be useful
as it's been constructed?"
    I don't know if it matters. It is what it is
at this point. And I guess I'm more interested
in thinking about *Lovecraft Country,* for example,
as something that has like really blown a lot
of people's minds; all over Twitter, people are
like, how was it that there's monsters and ghosts
and the evilest thing on the show is still white
people? And I'm just like–we knew this!
...
    If we're stuck with race, I'm interested in
how we can use it to disrupt the ways that it
works in the world. With *Lovecraft,* for example,
if that's what it takes to get white people to
understand how evil historically they have been,
then, great.

On Design Pedagogy, Solutionism, and Critique

Organizer
[*Question from audience*] "Lauren you've mentioned how
design problem-solving → design is broadly understood as a problem-solving
practice. And this notion is being reinforced by
design education in a way that is often uncritical
and apolitical. I'm interested in how you counter
this notion in your teaching and what theories,
philosophies, pedagogies, etc., inform your
educational practice."

Lauren
Great question. This is my second year teaching,
and I've only really taught core studio so far.
I've found that in cases, for example, like design
research studio, where students are expected
to, in this particular case, research a topic

in Detroit that relates to some kind of social concern and then create something in response, the examples I give them are not solutions. Usually in that course, people will produce things that address homelessness or solve housing issues in Detroit, or do these massive projects that a nineteen-year-old is not going to resolve in a six-week project...

I try to introduce ways of working that are more about critical understanding or how you embed a critique in a thing that you make, whether it's a poster or a book or whatever. So that's one thing I try to do, steer students away from mediums or design objects that represent traditional solutions to problems.

And also, I don't use the same language in the classroom. I refuse to refer to things as "solutions." I did this today in a mixed studio with fine art students and graphic design students: To the graphic designers, I was like: "Do not produce a solution for this project. That is not what we're doing." It's just not. So, a lot of it's pretty upfront. I think a lot of it is informed by my own MFA education, which was pretty steeped in critical theory. (Shout out to Arden, who I think is on this call, who taught much of that coursework for me).

It's in my language, it's in the examples I give … I've changed around a "type one" class, for example, to make students go look for type and signage in Detroit—which is full of vernacular type all over the place. And I'm telling white students who mostly live in the suburbs to do this, by the way, because they never get out of their cars in the city, for the most part.

Black Joy as a Radical Act, and the Weaponization of Black Laughter

John

I was thinking about the National Memorial for Peace and Justice (in Montgomery, Alabama). Each of the obelisks represents someone who was lynched in a particular state; it has people's names on it, and states can actually get these sent to them. But essentially, it's a monument to tragedy, as well as a monument to healing, hopefully, which I find really interesting.

And then these jars that are in the church

that survived the Tulsa Race Massacre—these are
designed objects that hold the names and the
dirt where people were supposedly killed, because
they're still looking for the folks that were
murdered there too. So there are ways to talk
about how to give things form, but also about
the hope to heal through this particular form.
Because at the end of the day, for me, horror
is really about letting go of the trauma and
trying to move forward. I was thinking too about
what Lauren was talking about—different ideas
around waiting and what that does to someone,
how that changes something, how it actually
disrupts or mutates it.

I'm working on a horror story and thinking
about these things called laughing barrels.
Basically, during slavery time, even Black
people's joy and laughter were controlled. There
were these barrels that you would stick your
head in and laugh into. I think that's where they
get "a barrel of laughs" from. So, I had this
idea that this particular barrel was magical in
some way. And then these archeologists find it
many, many years later and what's happened is
all the laughter that's inside it has fermented... ← time; reassembling
it becomes something else. When it's let out, it
becomes this thing called the Side Splitter, and
it basically is weaponized as Black laughter.

Lauren
One thing related to that, which I'm thinking
about with the abolition project: my instinct is
that it's utopic for abolition to be a reality,
but I'm also sort of struggling with... I think I'm
more comfortable with creating a shitty horrific
scenario that reinforces some questions about
present reality, the future, and how we get there.
To me it's really hard to work through this in a
way that frames it as a set of possibilities or
opportunities, rather than use horror or dystopia
to drive a point home. And so a lot of it has
been imagining worst-case scenarios and then
trying to... but it's already so bad and it's just...
[laughter].

John
A lot of these types of traumatic things have
been swept under the rug, disrupted... I mean,
we already had multiple Wakandas, but they were

48

destroyed during the Red Summer. Or something that's equivalent to that. I mean, Tulsa was terrible... And by the way, Tulsa, Oklahoma, bounced right back. People don't talk about the fact that after the Tulsa Race Massacre [in the Greenwood District.], the community hunkered down and actually rebuilt almost immediately.

But there's also this idea of displaying Black suffering and Black spectacle. I happen to believe that Black joy is a radical act. But yeah, a lot of those histories have been disrupted. And even if you look at a Black speculative fiction from the Harlem Renaissance or earlier... When did Pauline Hopkins write *Of One Blood*? I think in the early-nineteen hundreds. It's about a Black man who goes to a hidden Ethiopian city that's very mystical, like Wakanda. So, there are these these constructions around utopic spaces that are already happening. And of course, my friend Stacy Robinson talks about this a lot too. We've also had Black utopias, or peaceful, loving spaces in music.

radical joy →

So whether it's "Ghetto Wonderland" or "Erotic City" or "Funky Town"... These are all heterotopic spaces that did exist in music... and that's something that Kodwo Eshun writes about in his book, *More Brilliant Than the Sun: Adventures in Sonic Fiction* (1998), where he talks about music as an escape pod or something like that, which Amiri Baraka also writes about in the short story "Rhythm Travel" (1995), where it's about time travel through music.

↖ pg.97

We can actually turn these ideas around design and race toward a more positive space, too. But there is something very cathartic about dealing with this darker affect, because it's the thing that's been given to us. 'Cause it's not like we came out of a womb saying, "Oh, hello, I'm Black." It was like, "No, here's a Black identity." And then you figure out the rest of your life, how to deal with it, and the same thing with whiteness too. All this stuff is storytelling, different types of narratives that just get reinforced.

← cathartic/ healing

...

I turn fifty next week—which is wonderful—I'm happy to be here, happy to be a dad, happy to do the stuff I'm doing. But I also think about the fact that Black men from my generation were statistically not supposed to, live past twenty-

five years old... So the idea that I've lived
twice as long as I was supposed to is wonderful
and frightening. I always feel like I'm living
on borrowed time and trying to create a better
future that I probably won't live to see. And
that's the thing too. You're sowing seeds for
the future.

I often think about Derrick Bell's *Faces at
the Bottom of the Well: The Permanence of Racism*
(Basic Books, 1992)—the idea of being stuck
at the bottom of the well. My friend Rinaldo
Anderson was talking about how, the way you get

collectivity; affective connection → out of the well is to actually stand on each
other's shoulders to get out. Somebody gets out
at the end of it, but you don't know. It's not

inertia (waiting) → going to be you. It might not be me, but maybe
it will be my son. Maybe it'll be his son. These
systems were put in place a long time ago and

mechanism of maintenance → they are extremely well-designed. I kind of admire
their design—stereotypes function very well.

As a designer I admire that, but what happens
to the folks that these particular systems are
being placed upon? For instance, the character
The Dark—that muzzle he had—they used to put
that on escaped slaves, because what it would do
is that it would catch on branches and stuff, and
it would make sounds so that you could catch them.
That's really smart. It's really well designed.
But it also destroys families. It is actually
a manifestation of a particular type of system.
Those are the things I'm talking about. Those
images of slave ships with the little slave bodies
up in there—those things are measured out really
well and they function. Or the tenements and
projects, those are all design systems.

But they are also extremely soul crushing
and don't take into account the affect of what
happens. That's something that I'm trying to get
at, the affect. That's why I think we're still
attracted to horror, because horror is the thing
that's after the terrible thing has happened.
It's affect—it's the thing you're left with.

The Actual Function of Design
as Opposed to How It's Posited as a Problem-Solving Tool

Lauren
I don't think I believe design is a problem-
solving tool. The people who designed race, not

designers, you know. I've talked a lot about this moment in history in the 1400s when this Portuguese guy—I think his name was Gomes Eanes de Zurara—was like, "I really want to extract more money from my trade of slaves. How do I do this? I need to negate the human value of the middlemen I'm working with. Let me commission a report about how barbaric Africans are." He commissioned race. I don't think it actually requires designers. I don't think that design, the way that I've learned it, is a particular problem-solving tool. I'll just offer some examples.

I think design makes forms, for example, into very literal things. It makes things real that people might not have seen before, occupying their world. Whether that's a two-dimensional visual image of something or an experience in space. So, to the extent that it does that, sure, it could solve some kind of problem. But my issue with design being framed in that way is that the way design resolves things is usually cosmetic. It makes us think that something is possible, but it doesn't get us to the possibilities, if that makes sense. Especially in thinking about these big questions… what I'm talking about requires revolution. I can imagine it and I can design it and make it seem real, but it is literally going to require revolutions. And that is not a designed act. That's a completely different set of actions.

design problem-solving →

51

Interview with
Lauren Williams

Both of you explore the expanded notions
of design—as a space for the mythical and
spiritual, which are often excluded from
mainstream design—and play with existing
genres, such as science fiction and
corporate branding, to engage in critical
speculation and world-building. How does this
strategic misuse enter design pedagogy?

Sept. 2022

Lauren My entire orientation to design as a field of study and practice emerged from *outside* the field, so I've probably been,
in a sense, "misusing" it (strategically or un-strategically) since
I first began. Before I entered the design field, I had been doing
policy, research, and program management targeted at helping
low-income families build wealth and economic security. In this
role, I was swept up in the wave of design thinking's populariza-
← popular-
ization
of design
thinking
tion and became enamored by the promise of what I *thought* design thinking could offer the nonprofit industrial complex and all
↖ pg.128
its paternalistic baggage: a chance—I hoped—to listen intently to
the audiences we were designing policy and programs for and invite them in as co-designers of "solutions" to address the impediments preventing them from achieving the economic mobility
they'd been promised.
    I was introduced to the world of design from a position
in which I understood it only as another means of advancing a
particular kind of social change I was interested in. I came to
understand its more "mainstream" applications in a roundabout
way. Along the way, thankfully, I was disabused of the naïve hope
I initially (mis)placed in design thinking to shift centuries-long

patterns of disinvestment, theft, and exploitation by churning out quippy "solutions." I did, however, come to understand that design—broadly interpreted as manipulating materials, forms, and spaces to shape an experience—paired with a critical orientation and a deeper political foundation, could also offer a set of tools for asking crucial questions about why social fictions like racism prevail, why capitalism is so hard to change, and why we continue to distribute power so unevenly. Beyond that, I came to understand it as a tool for "imagining otherwise," to borrow from Christina Sharpe.

This is the orientation I bring to classrooms. Most of the time, that has meant somewhat surreptitiously trying to counter some degree of what I know is the mainstream pedagogy surrounding me, to which students have already been indoctrinated. That has meant tweaking a thesis studio to reinforce the notion that we are all bringing some semblance of our positioning in the world (identity, geography, beliefs) to whatever we design; driving home the myth of "neutrality." This started with students recovering a sense of themselves they'd been taught, in large part, to obscure as designers—we started with bell hooks on self-recovery—before initiating their self-directed thesis work. In a first-year type course, it looked like bringing the political geography of the city we're situated in—Detroit, Michigan—into an assignment; inviting students to engage with the city they study in (but rarely experience) by searching for and tracing hand-painted signage in order to learn the mechanics of local typography.

To sum it up, I think I'm most interested in using design to *do other things that fail to deliver on its capacity to serve capital*: to question the political geography of Detroit, to uncover and recover parts of ourselves, to critique oppression. So, my operative mode tends to be a stubbornly strategic misuse of the practice, particularly in classrooms where pedagogy prioritizes preparing students for industry.

projection
of social
fictions →

↖ pg. 117

(myth of)
neutrality →

↖ pg. 113

design,
design
profession →

xpectations
 schooling →

53

If we accept that design gives form, legibility, and availability to the invisible, intangible, and abstract (that it designates, in short), your work engages this through the formal representation of oppression as designed artifacts, pushing on definitions of race, designation, as something that is "real." John (Jennings), for instance, creates neologisms and characters, and engages in world-building; Lauren, your work gives form and materiality to intangible concepts such as rage.

Legibility can be double-edged—race is designed as a tool for making certain bodies legible in order to manage a population. On the other hand, being able to name one's oppressor, to identify a grievance when enslaved people were denied the right to read and write, makes language appear as an emancipatory vocation (Paulo Freire might call this "naming the world.")

What values do you see in designing something into legibility or illegibility? When do we want to be seen or unseen, and how does design play a role in this?

Lauren My work on Black rage felt like a more personal pursuit than usual, like it was something I needed to process for myself as I thought about how to situate myself in movement spaces, in white institutions, and in the world, all at once. This isn't to say I never considered who would *consume* the work and how they might read it, but I suppose I made it because *I needed to make it,* first and foremost. I knew that it was legible to me but didn't really know or care if it would be legible to anyone else (Black or otherwise). I wondered, at first: If I make this material, if I give it form, can I shape it differently? Can it shape me differently? A part of me wonders, though, if what I created actually made Black rage *any more legible* to anyone other than me—or if it was just another cryptic expression of a feeling that I struggle to articulate even though it is integral and ever-present in *all* my work and much of my life. I'm also cognizant that, at the end of the day, white people are busy making up their own narratives around Black rage—and countless other "illegible" things about Black experiences and aliveness and death—so, why not shape the narrative with my own contribution?

← material condition of Black Rage

54

In 2021, I began a body of work called *Wake Work*: Experiments in Black Redaction and Annotation*, in which I was explicitly

← pg.98 concerned with rendering Black suffering *illegible*. This body of work examines violences visited on Black people at the hands of the American state and attends to the paradoxes of Black life and death in this anti-Black world. In response to violent annotations and redactions made on Black lives by the police in all their forms, this work resists and refuses those terrors as captured in still images by employing "Black redaction and annotation." Departing from Sharpe's *In the Wake*, Black redactions and an-

re-assembling → notations reveal new ways of seeing the systems made visible in these images and the violences those systems enact. Further, this work examines the absurdity of what emerges from the wake when calls to redress systems that deliver anti-Black terror are met with empty, performative remedies.

My process began with literally dissecting images depicting violence against Black people, starting with documentation of Haitian migrants being brutalized as they attempted to cross the US-Mexico border and expanding to other instances of police brutalizing Black people in the US throughout time. In this case, I saw design as offering a set of material and formal tactics for both critiquing these moments but also forcing a kind of illegibility through Black redaction and annotation. I was hyper-aware of how retraumatizing it would be to confront *other Black people* with these images and what it would mean to serve them up to the predominantly white crowd that would inevitably view the show in its first installment (at a major university gallery). This was a case where, with the aid of Sharpe's text, I sought to reshape the source material in a way that forced a different view, compromised the legibility of Black suffering, and demanded that viewers sit reverently with the material in the way one might sit at a *wake* with a dying family member.

In Sharpe's words, "Black redaction and...annotation are ways of imagining otherwise." To that end, this work reshapes ways of seeing terror and timelessness captured in photos of anti-Black state violence. Such experiments create disturbances, ← re-assembling open wounds, and produce wakes in these representations of Black people in distress by cutting away at images; recomposing them; transforming them into new, abstract, dimensional objects; viewing them through the lens of critical texts; and treating those texts as both material and frame. This process poses questions about anti-Blackness, the optics of state violence, and the empty gestures to redress harm, temporality, and consciousness. ↖ pg.108

> Considering the idea that racialization is an instrument of European colonialism and coloniality, while also remembering that "post-raciality" is an innovation of white supremacy, how might designers address organizing or creating around race as the "master's tool"? What could subverting the master's tool consist of?

Lauren Race and post-raciality aren't real, yes. *But*, racism and the contingent effects of both our racialization and the fallout from the misperception that we live in a post-racial world very much *are real.* For this reason, I struggle with categorizing Black designers, specifically, as wielding a "master's tool" when organizing or creating around or in response to race in their own work.

Every single designer is designing *from and around* "who they are"—including and especially white folks or hetero folks or cisgender folks or non-immigrants or able-bodied folks—but we never deign to ask them these questions. We presume a designer's so-called neutrality until we glimpse an identifiable sense of difference or marginality. But race and racism shape cultural expressions, family norms, and shared experience; race becomes a marker through which we identify with or distance ourselves from other people. So, when a designer makes work around race because who they are affords them a critical lens on something unseen by those without their racialized experi-

56

ence, that feels—if we must call it so—like a worthy repurposing of a "master's tool." Wielding race as a clearer, more refined lens through which to see and critique the world *isn't the same tool* as the instrument of race used to categorize, exploit, and exclude people under capitalism, for example. Or, when a designer makes work around race because they want to reclaim some part of themselves they've been compelled to withhold, that feels like a worthy reclaiming of a "master's tool."

re-
assembling →

As an aside, I don't think all artists or designers who make work in which their racialized identity is central necessarily believe that their work will, for example, topple racism (or "dismantle the master's house," as hooks put it). To be more precise, *I think many designers make work around race for reasons other than* "dismantling the master's house." I would posit instead that they may be creating around race in order to make sense of their everyday racialized reality, or to see more work that connects to them because we deserve to be *represented* in the ways we want to be seen. We seem to place undue pressure on racialized designers to do the work of undoing racism, when what they need or desire, instead, might be the freedom to make the work that feels truest to them. In constructing race, white supremacists scavenged corporeal and cultural parts of us and assigned to them derision and condemnation and derogation: a Black designer making work from a place that uplifts those same parts of themselves may not be utilizing the "master's tool" of race so much as reclaiming parts of themselves *taken* or denigrated by the construction of race in the first place.

↖ pg.98

material
ndition of
esentation
nd erasure →

labor →

↖ pg.107

projection →

In contemplating whether a "master's tool" is at work here, however, the lingering question I return to, is: Does that designer creating work around their race make some quality of their identity more consumable, palatable, or profitable for the machine of racial capitalism or neoliberalism in the process? Are they (inadvertently or not) using the tools of a racist patriarchy to prop up that racist patriarchy?

⟋ profitability
of design;
accountability
/complicity

In this formula of designers-making-work-around-race, the operative master's *tool* I see doing the lion's share of the work is *design*, not race. *Design* as we know it is a practice that pre- ← design profession dominantly serves capital, absent some miracle or repurposing or "strategic misuse," as you named in an earlier question. Is it possible, then, to "strategically misuse" design in a way that upsets or defangs its capacity to serve racial capitalism? This is a selfish framing, of course, because I would attempt to situate my own work in such a way that—at a minimum—design is *not* being leveraged to further feed into racial capitalism. It would take a much more substantial transformation of the means by which I produce this work and the ways in which I share the wealth it generates and the comforts it affords me to substantiate a true subversion of the instrument of design. But, at the very least, we might ask, can a racialized person's critical eye and hand and chosen applications of design, for example, transform the tool into something new? What if their design is divorced from some ← structural agency of designer profit-making and -hoarding endeavor altogether?

> How do you think about criticism of ← speculation/imagination
> speculative design fiction—such as those
> dystopian scenarios where the "fiction"
> is already someone else's reality? Does
> designing close to, with, and for the
> oppressed, counter this dynamic? Is
> speculative design a useful category for
> describing such practices?

Lauren I see those criticisms as pretty accurate. Speculative design can come across as paternalistic when it catastrophizes and fetishizes collapse or disaster surrounding issues that people are already suffering in today's world. A lot of speculative design is deeply techno-solutionist at a time when it's more apparent ← design problem- solving than ever that technology can't save us from ourselves. Still, compelling storytelling—some of which employs speculative fiction and designed objects—can be powerful. Seeing, holding, turning

58

over, or standing within tangibly different worlds—as facilitated by design mediums—can help people see their own realities in a new light, understand urgencies and pitfalls more viscerally, and grasp our role in seemingly intangible futures in an uncanny way. After watching the dystopian crisis of COVID-19 unfold, however, motivating *zero* substantial, long-term shifts in the US in terms of how we care for each other and how we think about collective well-being, labor, public health, and the commitments to each other required to preserve it, I'm feeling pretty cynical about the capacity for even the most compelling "cautionary tales" to result in any sort of actual transformation. That said, I still have some (perhaps misguided) hope that, yes, shining a light on the futures we might face through speculative design could be a motivating force for shifting the ways we move through the world *today*.

I think designing close to and with oppressed and marginalized folks might address some of this dynamic, but I'm still skeptical. Doing so requires, first of all, that we know *how* to design "with" and "for," which I don't think most designers do. I struggle with it myself even though collaboration and a generative participatory process are a central part of my practice. Many of the techniques I've learned through design or social science research methods for engaging *any* other people in the practice of design maintain a degree of extraction and paternalism that's ↖ pg. 128 hard to shake (try as I might).

Instead of trying to shift speculative design, one opportunity here may be to begin to make space within *speculative design* to acknowledge the forms of design that emerge from places of marginalization and oppression that rarely get acknowledged as such. Or, we have another opportunity to think about how speculative design could *modify* or complement other fields of practice: for example, from where I sit today, I'm most interested in speculative design's capacity to enable and advance commuollective action → nity organizing work. In that endeavor, I think design needs to take a backseat to organizing and the relational work that makes

59

organizing possible. In other words—and maybe this is too slight a distinction of semantics or orientation, but one I find worth making—(speculative) design simply doesn't have the range to lead here; it cannot so easily shed its baggage and escape its lineage. But, maybe (hopefully, selfishly), alongside an organizing community or political home, (speculative) design can morph into a thing that caters less to its masters and more to the interests of community, whatever form that may take.

I find myself bouncing back and forth in an extremely noncommittal way to find language to name what I do that falls into this category of speculative design. Depending on who I'm talking to, I might call it futurism, critical design, or design fiction. In most cases, I'm just trying to avoid sounding pretentious about what I'm doing or aligning myself with a category that feels too narrow or limiting, especially if I'm talking to non-designers. If I'm making a bunch of made-up, fictional artifacts, maybe it's just more legible and meaningful to say that *I'm making a bunch of fictional objects from the future.*

> Do you see the speculative objects in your ← speculation/imagination
> project as thought experiments that are
> never meant to be realized, or as visions
> of alternative worlds? If the diegetic
> prototypes speak to a closed circle, and a
> certain level of literacy is required to be
> able to "read" the objects, does the work
> need to be explained to a larger audience?
> How do you build that audience? How do
> these objects circulate? Do they disseminate
> through exhibition mechanisms, as art, or
> through existing forms of dissemination of
> design? (And how might we see this through
> the lens of the known/unknown and legibility/
> illegibility?)

Lauren I see speculative objects as thought experiments, not visions: *provocations* is the word I've used, of late, to describe these when they show up in my work. This is true of *Tribute* (2019), the work I shared during our talk in 2020. It's also true of a project

60

called *Making Room for Abolition* (2021), for which I recently constructed a larger design fiction—a (Black family's) living room from a Detroit without police and prisons.

In both cases, I *did not* want to convey these as visions. With *Tribute*, a fiction in which local council members are controlled by constituents via Tamagotchi-like devices, the operative provocation was: What changes about policymakers' relationships to power when constituents on the receiving end of their policymaking control their physiological well-being? How does this change the stakes? To be clear, there is nothing good about this scenario, but the provocation might shift the way we think about the motivations behind policymaking *today*.

With *Making Room for Abolition*, the operative provocation was: What would have to shift about our everyday lives to make possible a world without police and prisons? What evidence would we find in our homes of these shifts? I was concerned with making sure that this wouldn't be perceived as a vision for some kind of utopic abolitionist future scenario where rainbows and butterflies proliferate and police and prisons vanish and everyone lives happily ever after. In the futures represented in this space, there's a different geography, the water crises we face in Detroit have evolved, there are news stories that depict how messy the fallout from police abolition might be, the types of monuments that will be erected to memorialize policing are debated, and so on.

In the case of *Making Room for Abolition*, the objects circulated through a private art gallery; in the case of *Tribute*, they were accessible only through an installation in a graduate school gallery. I'm frustrated by the limitations of these platforms and have been thinking through better ways of making these narratives available to people who have a stake in seeing them realized *and* what will happen if they aren't. With *Making Room for Abolition*, my underlying, long-term intention was to begin considering what it would take to use futuring as an organizing tool toward abolishing police and prisons. Typically, this kind of futurism is levied against us in the context of policing: popular media have given us more futuristic police, more police technologies, and more entrenched relationships between capital and the state that make it easier and more seamless for police to control and oppress folks. So, dissemination here feels more urgent and—as the work continues—it's clear that a gallery can't be the space for that work to live and evolve.

Legibility and reach seem to contradict each other in this kind of work. I was reminded of this at the opening of *Making Room for Abolition*: hundreds of people flooded the gallery bearing drinks and hollering to be heard over one another. What people will take away from a show like *Making Room* really depends on how much they're going to engage with the minutiae that surround them; the story was buried in the dozens of artifacts placed about the "living room," but amid the din and the bustle of the party, focusing on these objects was a challenge. Sure, folks may return during gallery hours later on, come back for a tour and conversation with the artist another day, or read the pamphlets available upon entering for more context. Regardless of whether they came on opening night or after, it's hard to know if people will leave with the takeaway that "the future is purple!" or if they'll stop and ask why the grandmother loved playing cards so much—a note they'd only find by reading her obituary placed with care next to her memory jug.

I've thought about the need to turn this work into a narrative piece that people can better follow through short films or audio pieces. I've struggled, in part, because I'm afraid of concretizing them as fixed narratives—I want them to live as provocations, to be used to generate other stories, as jumping-off points, as points for conversation, not as predictions about alternative worlds. To this end, when *Making Room for Abolition* was open, I invited a few groups of Detroit-based organizers, educators, gardeners, teachers, and others to visit the space and hold

Lauren Williams

recorded conversations about the questions the room and its artifacts provoked for them *in real life*. This was my early attempt at extending the life of the discourse beyond the gallery; sometime in 2023, these recordings will see the light of day. During the process of making this work, too, I invited about thirty Detroiters to critique and workshop some of the early artifacts I had begun making: a transformative justice summons, lawn signs, news headlines, a guaranteed income check, and more. Both of these settings—which asked others to interpret the objects for themselves—highlighted the fact that *misreads* of the artifacts were also telling and valuable in their own way; sometimes they revealed the questions *really* clawing at people, questions I hadn't yet conceived of. Sure, it feels validating for the work to be "understood" in those moments when someone paces carefully through the installation and realizes the connections between thoughtful details on objects you spent weeks crafting. But there's a different, more generative, and—perhaps more honest—kind of validation in being misunderstood in a way that reminds you that there are no guarantees, and the lenses folks bring to your work will inevitably expand the potential significance of what you've made (or remind you to take yourself a little less seriously).

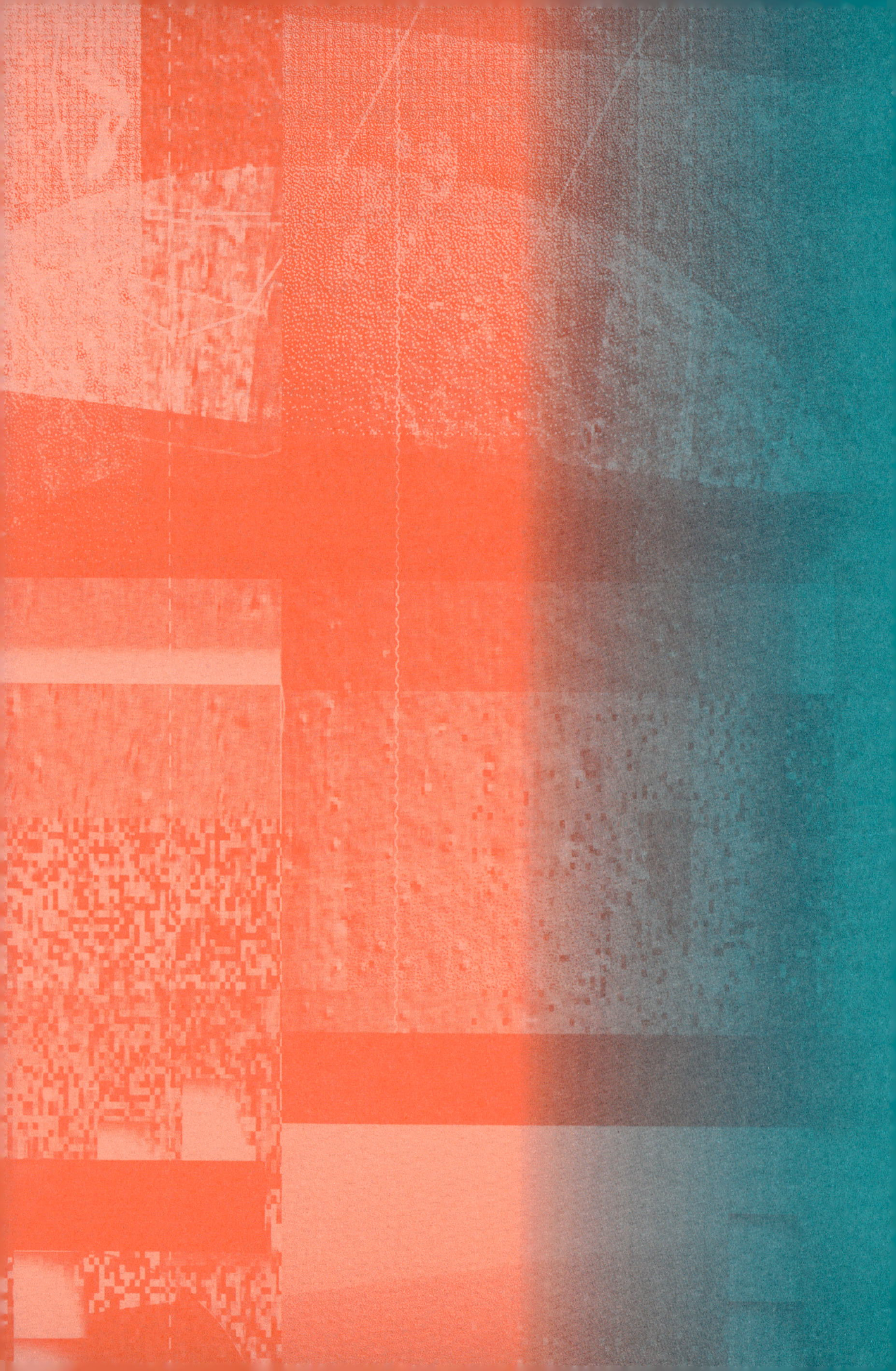

Cosmopolitanism and Difference in Design Language: Some Reflections on the Decolonial Turn from Pakistan

Ahmed Ansari

Jun 2022

"Authenticity"

In March 2021, Imran Khan's government introduced the first wave of education reforms aimed at bridging the historical disparities that had marked Pakistan's various systems of education—separated along provincial lines—under the mandate of the Single National Curriculum (SNC), which, as the Ministry of Federal Education and Professional Training (MFEPT) claimed, was aimed at "one system of education for all, in terms of curriculum, medium of instruction and a common platform of assessment, so that all children have a fair and equal opportunity to receive high quality education."

Much has been written about the deep inequities of contemporary Pakistani education (Rahman, 2004; Idrees and Shah, 2018), which is divided between the private sector that follows the British GC(S)E system, wherein the medium of instruction is English; the public "Metric" or "Intermediate" school system, where instruction is in Urdu or provincial languages; and the "madrassah" system, the network of traditional schools providing free Islamic education in any number of regional vernacular languages.

All three systems diverge greatly in terms of content and structure, sometimes to the point of incommensurability. What's more, there is a great disparity in the quality of teachers, administration, and infrastructure between all three systems, and they suffer from a disconnect between

the priorities agenda of the school and nation →

curricula and social-cultural realities when it comes to who is allowed to attend school (particularly along the lines of gender difference), who learns and find themselves reflected in their education (language, ethnicity, and culture), and who can attend what kind of school (class).

The justification that the Pakistani prime minister provided on August 25, 2021, in an address to the Punjab Education Convention, was not inaccurate: the education system is deeply fractured, and its own inequities are symptomatic of, and contribute to, larger social inequalities. Nor was Imran Khan's attribution of a bifurcated education system dividing society along distinct class lines to the colonial period of British rule inaccurate: colonial authorities in the early-mid nineteenth century did indeed institute the first universities, where Anglophone education was intended to create a new class of local bureaucrats hailing largely from the existing upper castes and classes, and receiving great support from leading Indian intellectuals and educational reformers of the day such as Ram Mohan Roy (Sangwan 1985) and Syed Ahmed Khan (Belmekki 2009).

← the priorities/agenda of the school and nation

Imran Khan and the Pakistan-Tehreek-e-Insaf (PTI) party's proposal for a unified curriculum with the goal of "decolonizing" the education system from its colonial legacy (Khoja-Moolji 2017; Tahir, 2022), should be read within a larger context of advocacy and discourse around the present regime's claims of taking an "anti-imperialist" stance against Westernization. One can find this most explicitly articulated in the Khan government's recent creation of the Rahmatul-lil-Alameen Authority in October 2021, tasked with countering what the regime termed the kind of general moral decline in Pakistan's youth due to the proliferation of foreign influences, largely from the Anglo-European world (Dawn 2021).

What, though, is the content of this project? A comprehensive document outlining the vision for the course of study provides details of a year-long process undertaken to develop the curriculum: interestingly, the input of the Ittehad-e-Tanzeemat-Madaras Pakistan, the largest representative body for the thousands of madrasahs across Pakistan, was consulted in tandem with the University of Cambridge. Just as in the process that created it, the outlined goals of the SNC also revealed stark contradictions: the teachings of the Quran and Sunnah are cited as a principal goal in addition to analytical, critical, and creative thinking, and Islamiat is integrated as a core component of the curriculum in grades 1–12 (non-Muslims, instead of taking "Ethics," are now required to take a course called "Religious Education").

A closer look at the visual and rhetorical strategy in the textbooks written for primary schoolkids further illustrates what "decolonisation" in Imran Khan's government looks like: the cover of a grade 5 English textbook shows a mother and her daughter dressed in local kurtas, wearing headscarves, and sitting on the floor reading, while the father and son sit above them on a sofa bedecked in shirts and jeans. They are, presumably, a Sunni family—the headscarves are white—and they are most certainly Muslim (there are no Hindu, Christian, Sikh, Parsi, Jain, Buddhist, or, lord forbid, atheist or agnostic families in Pakistan). The illustrations are also shorn of any ethnic signifiers or evidence of vernacular culture, in fact: since this is a national curriculum, to show anyone as Sindhi, Punjabi, Balochi, Pashtun,

\ (myth of) neutrality

Balti, Kashmiri, Muhajir, etc. would defeat the point.

Ironically, these images illustrate a picture of Pakistan that mirrors the kinds of images of "authentic" Islamicate culture and society that have so dominated the imaginaries of the Anglo-European world and circulated in the West—images that the postcolonial scholar Edward Said famously critiqued in his book, *Orientalism* (Said ← projection 1978): Islamicate societies appear as homogenous, monocultural, backward societies, perpetually caught in a sort of limbo between tradition and modernity. Clearly, Pakistani bureaucrats and educators seem to view their societies in much the same way their American and European interlocutors have: not, as the Sri Lankan anthropologist Gananath Obeyesekere argued in his famous 1992 debate with Marshall Sahlins (Obeyesekere, 1992; Sahlins, 1995), as equal torchbearers of the values the European Enlightenment claimed to exemplify, but as absolutely, ← many incommensurately different from the West, other and their absolute alterity must be respected and maintained. centers and peripheries

I am not going to dwell much longer on the myriad critiques of the SNC from educators and intellectuals throughout the country, which have cropped up since its introduction. Suffice to say that these local critiques, among other things, point to the disparities between what the SNC claims to do and what its content actually reflects. Most of all, they signal the SNC's failure to properly frame and remedy a panoply of structural features that are just as, if not more, important, than the content of what children learn in school: a lack of schools, instructors, and infrastructure; the unaffordable costs of school for the working classes; the lack of accessibility across gender and regions, and so forth. None of these structural features seem to have changed throughout Imran Khan's tenure, which has sought to remake the content of education while leaving its larger structural and infrastructural problems ← cosmetic untouched. change /empty gestures

66

In fact, if anything, new practices outline the structure of a disciplinary regime that has emerged during the present government's tenure. A recent piece by Pervez Hoodbhoy—a physicist and vocal critic of the growing Deobandi Islamization of public institutions and general publics—showed how the enforcement of the SNC has now produced new grounds for the surveillance and disciplining of school principals and teachers who deliver the curriculum, and for making sure that learning to recite the Quran is being done "properly." As Hoodbhoy states, "magistrates accompanied by rifle-bearing policemen are pouncing upon schools, interrogating 7 to 12 year-old children" (Hoodbhoy 2021). The piece, published days after a mob of factory workers in Sialkot tortured and murdered their Sri Lankan floor manager (Al Jazeera 2021), speaks volumes about larger shifts towards ever-more extreme performances of religio-nationalism sanctioned under the present regime.

"Hybridity"
Arriving in Karachi this winter after an almost four-year absence, I found that decolonisation had traveled across the world and taken root in local discourse and practice: local faculty wanted me to talk about it, while their students were engaged in doing projects on it. I saw two graduating student theses at the Indus Valley School of Art and Architecture (IVSAA) explicitly use the term and wrap themselves in its claims. One student explained to me how her interest in developing signage systems based on local languages had led her to discover that the largely rural, peasant, and working-class patients at the hospital made sense of visual form in ways very different from urban, literate, Western(ized) subjects. Her work took me back to my own observations about vernacular visual grammars in studies conducted over 2013 and 2014, when I examined hospital signage systems in Karachi—observations that first set me

on my own path to interrogate and understand more deeply cultural difference and change. Perhaps there is some significance in the fact that it is with critiques of the incomprehensibility of the most "global" of graphic systems—i.e., isotype—that local graphic designers start their journeys toward developing an attentiveness, a sensitivity, to different visual epistemologies. ← many other centers and peripheries

But to return to the students' thesis presentations, I found it both encouraging and alarming that, even as they were trying to understand and translate the differences they found in local, vernacular languages, the language they used to articulate the premise of their projects was completely foreign (or perhaps, "global"): it was the language used by academics in the United States to describe *their* projects of decolonisation. What also disturbed me, although I could not quite articulate this at the time, was the unproblematized, uncritical taking up of Urdu as a language *indigenous* to Pakistan—a very troubled claim in the long history of ethnic tensions around language and the use of language by the state as a tool for minoritization and political control through Pakistan's existence.

And I thought, yet again, how urgent it is that design studies scholars question the terms under which concepts and their use travel and change across the globe, and what, if any, relations of Anglocentric onto-epistemic domination they produce. I thought that *this*—the global movement of language, concepts, and practices—should also open up questions around things we've taken for granted—questions about what modernity is and what it means to be modern, in the sense of what modernity *opens us up to* in addition to what it (fore)closes. What kinds of subjects does globalization make of us? What happens when foreign ontologies take root in faraway lands? Despite so ← in-betweener many years of traveling back and forth between Pakistan and the United States, I have never been able to make up my mind about whether Pakistani design education is too closeted and provincial, too used

Cosmopolitanism and Difference...

to engaging with its own issues within its own narrow sense of the immediate world and the horizon of its historical and institutional affinities, or whether it is global in the truest sense of the word, often incorporating and transmuting ideas, practices, and tools from outside into recognisable but nevertheless new forms.

My own undergraduate education at the same school was a curious blend of the traditional and the modern, the local and foreign. Most of the exercises and projects we did in class had first been derived in Europe, and I'm not entirely sure to what extent they were modified from their original formulations. On average, for every semester of graphic design and typography studio, perhaps two to three weeks were devoted to local typography, and even then, only in Urdu, the national language. The few liberal arts courses there were, were largely on American and European art and design history, but we did spend one semester learning about Islamicate art and architecture. The curricula changed but little over the years, and we learned nothing of the changes and shifts in design discourse and practice that moved through America or Europe, much less the rest of the world—the history we read seemed, well, stuck in history. What we learned of design abroad largely came indirectly through the internet; no one in Karachi seemed involved in global discussions or debates.

All of our instructors spoke English; there was, especially coming from the founders of the school and the senior faculty, a distinctly bourgeois air about the place, and many of them spoke in crisply enunciated, vaguely British-sounding accents. Pedagogically, there was a strain of the (colonial?) "strict schoolmaster"-style of teaching that seems to have gone out of fashion in the last few decades in US academia, although it certainly did exist there too, judging from the horror stories one hears from students of Paul Rand: stern and inaccessible demeanors, an emphasis on discipline and punishment

through tight deadlines and high standards, critique styles largely focusing on faults and frailties and very little on what students do well, a certain wariness of breaking convention or departing from instructor expectations, and a constant reinforcement of the image of the instructor as "the master" in a master-apprentice system. Clearly, no one then (or now) had read Ivan Illich.

But there were other, more benevolent dimensions to it too. Our teachers did encourage in us, sometimes in even crisper Urdu, a love of local art, craft, and tradition. For one of our culminating projects in freshman year, we had the choice of adapting and putting on a play or producing a short film based on a piece of subcontinental fiction. We studied Urdu calligraphy alongside English typography for four semesters. The school regularly hosted events celebrating local culture— sometimes it was classical music, sometimes folk theater—and many of our assignments involved making trips into the city. There is no doubt in my mind that what the school represented was something as local as it was foreign, as much shaped by the city and country and its influences as it was by colonial ones. In almost every course and assignment, we were pushed to think about local design, even if we were focusing mostly on aesthetics and form.

Perhaps a better way of framing the work that the students produce in Pakistan is that it is something hybrid, engaging with and speaking of a world to which they do-but-not-quite belong in their largely English-educated, middle-class sensibilities, which nevertheless deals with everyday reality in Karachi and understands and interprets it in ways that no foreign tourist or Western academic could. What they produce in school and later, for clients, isn't the sort of design that, for example, the largely informally trained designers working at Urdu newspapers like the *Jung* or *Nawa-e-Waqt* produce, nor are their sensibilities similar to the printers creating wedding invites and posters at Urdu Bazaar, yet what they produce is still irrevocably

expectations of schooling / mainstream pedagogy/ paternalistic baggage

← craft

← inbetween

Ahmed Ansari

Pakistani. And who is to say that the latter works are not hybrid either, that they do not navigate between the local and the global, as Western design trends and sensibilities seep into wedding card designs, often in response to the cosmopolitan demands of globe-trotting clients? If anything, upon appraising the work that Pakistani designers and design students are producing, the analysis of forms and content reveals that the nature of cultural (re)production through design reveals culture and language precisely as sites of continuous reduction, translation, and transformation, rather than the kind of pure and essentialized continuity that a shallow reading of decoloniality would emphasize.

many other centers and peripheries ↗

Vernaculars

In paying attention to the way that words work across US and Pakistani design contexts, the concepts they conceal and the dynamics they reveal, I am reminded of the very careful attention to language the visual cultural theorist Kajri Jain pays when she writes about why she settled on the idea and language of "vernacular"— rather than the "traditional," "native," "indigenous," or "local"—to describe Indian street calendar art as an exemplar of Indian modernity in her book, *Gods in the Bazaar*:

> Vernacularity is not pure, systemic, temporally primordial, or territorially bounded; it speaks to the heterogeneity of postcolonial idioms and forms of experience while addressing their contemporaneity and currency, and their implicitly subordinate relation to hegemonic forms of discourse and practice (in short, their subalternity). In the Indian instance it is particularly useful as a category that can be associated with location but is not tied to it, steering clear of both the valorization of the "Indian village" characterizing South Asian studies and cultural practice for the better part of the 20th century and the equally ideologically loaded "urban turn" being celebrated at the turn of the millennium. (Jain 2007, 14)

Jain's careful attentiveness to words reveals several things. Firstly:

words only mean things *in relation, and in relations of difference*. In this way, they have depth—they cannot simply be substituted for each other. Meaning, in itself, is not simply a matter of definition by convention—it is something that is felt, that resides outside the word itself and that can be located in the contexts in which it is found and to which it is addressed, perhaps, in analogous ways to how designers and architects talk of "fit." Vernacularity perhaps, as Jain feels, gives us the kind of experiential and expressive heterogeneity that fits well the plurality of the Indian past and present, without reducing identity to land, history, or essence in the way that the "native" or "indigenous" would. It does not create the same problems that "native" does, with its history steeped in British colonial distinctions between the racialized self/other, and even more so in the questions it raises around who can be considered native to the Indian subcontinent (are Muslims "natives," for example?). It also doesn't raise the same kinds of problems as "indigenous," given that the constellation of terms surrounding indigeneity in India—"adivasi" and "scheduled tribe," for instance—also have origins as colonial, and later modern, political and juridical categories. It speaks to the incredibly heterogeneous lives of material things that find themselves a part of the lives of all the different kinds of subjects one finds on the streets of India.

For me, the "vernacular" raises similar questions around Pakistani identity, where it seems to fit better than either native or indigenous: as a *muhajir*, whose grandparents arrived from India in the 1950s, thinking with the vernacular bypasses both the trauma of Partition and the itinerant memory of home, as well as the problematics of uneasy belonging that have always marked *muhajir* identity since the exiles arrived in India. In their place, it speaks more of assimilation, of an expansive and positive belonging that has contributed to the patchwork of cultures that constitute the Pakistani nation. This, of course, also means that words *do* things (and have the capacity to do many different things). Nativity and indigeneity are not just concepts employed in discourses of emancipation; they find themselves at home in discourses of cultural exceptionalism and the politics of cultural purification. "Culture" itself, being in relation to the former two words, is defined as that which is essential, unchanging—not the expression of difference but an ideal to which subjects conform.

I believe that it is no coincidence that certain words and concepts like "decolonisation" have the capacity to be employed within very different political projects all around the world. In fact, that they do so should open us up to inquire more deeply as to what lends itself, in them, to different meanings and projects, and in doing so transforms the larger constellation of language that we find also implied, if not expressed, in our discourses. One could say, of course, that the kinds of political practices taken up by regimes like the Pakistani state (and one can certainly find parallels in, for example, India, Brazil, and China) are *not* decolonization—that they have nothing to do with the kinds of goals espoused by groups working toward greater inclusion and representation; fairer, more equitable pay; more just structures, etc. that are sweeping workplaces in the US right now, or the staunch activisms of Indigenous groups in the Americas and many other parts of the world fighting against states for greater autonomy and sovereignty.

But I would argue that perhaps it *is* important to take the claims of such regimes seriously. When we use words like "decolonisation" or "indigenous" in academic papers and presentations, and employ them in claims and projects, we should first ask ourselves, with as much attention as we pay to fit in questions of designed things, whether our words fit who we are and represent, who we are speaking to, where we are speaking and speaking from, what our particular sense of

a concept does to other related concepts, and how these make up our unquestioned assumptions. In fact, I believe that it is essential and crucial that designers take these matters of inquiry as central to any projects with ambitions and claims of decolonisation, because, as I have repeatedly emphasized in prior works, *decolonisation means different things for different people and contexts*. In cosmopolitan milieus and places, like in the North American classroom, where different subjects coexist and share the same space, the question of what it can mean collectively for them becomes especially pertinent.

I must confess that it is with more than a bit of dismay and sadness that I have witnessed much of the discourse around decolonisation in design skip over this vital inquiry: indeed, I would argue that the critique of Anglocentrism coming out of the early years of the decolonial turn has been frustrated in its attempts to decenter discourses coming out of the United States and Western Europe. If anything, as my anecdote on the content of design discourse in Karachi above attempts to show, the very US-centric language and conceptual framings of decolonisation, with their particular emphasis on very US-specific understandings of race, culture, indigeneity, ← projection etc., have a tendency to travel quickly over global circuits of information exchange and dominate local understandings. My fear is that this form of domination is enabled through twenty-first-century communication technologies, mediums, and genres, which in themselves constitute a form of epistemic colonialism that precludes the capacity for local discourses to develop on their own terms. I must confess that I am not quite settled on whether this fear is substantial or unfounded. It emerges from an intimate understanding of the historical frailties and failings of art and design education in Pakistan, of the effects of epistemic colonization.

My best hopes for Pakistani design academia have always involved it opening itself up to the world; but in an odd mirror,

Ahmed Ansari

my time teaching in the United States has given me the impression that things are not much different here; apart from its immigrants, perhaps, the American design community knows, and cares to know, little about the rest of the world and its immense multitudes. As the historian Dipesh Chakraborty articulated so well in *Provincializing Europe*, US design scholars, regardless of their racial or ethnic background, still feel no need, no urgency, to learn, learn from, and think through and from, other languages, histories, contemporary contexts, and ways of thinking and feeling (Chakraborty 2000).

labor → It is my observation, and again, this perhaps invites challenging, that the burden of labor in providing non-US accounts of design

↖ pg.57, 107, 119 largely falls on immigrant designers, design educators, and students. This reliance on immigrant accounts is also not without its problems, for it glosses over the issue of the reliability of immigrant interlocution: it assumes that immigrant scholars and students have "done their homework" in critically thinking through their own subject-positions and being careful about their translations of their root cultures. These are systemic problems global in scope that manifest within the US design academy and require significant changes in how we educate designers, especially graduate students aspiring to produce research that others will read and learn from. In any case, the pluriversality that now permeates the speech of designers can only remain an espoused commitment—never fully realized—whereas in reality, US design practice, scholarship, and education still remain very much parochial (Escobar 2018).

In my more cynical moments, I also entertain the important question of why US scholars need to engage with the work of

profit-ability of design → global others, particularly when the imperative in the field is to instrumentalize, to convert into use-value, the knowledge systems and perspectives of the latter. Given that the modern academy and institutions like universities and conservatories are themselves entirely compromised spaces

that exist to interpellate other knowledges and translate them into palatable and sanitized knowledge-capital (and I would refer parties interested in the fraught relationship between well-meaning academics aspiring to radical practice and fundamentally compromised academic institutions to Fred Moten and Stefano Harney's excellent essay, "The University and the Undercommons: Seven Theses"), perhaps it might be better to leave other knowledges alone (Moten and Harney 2004). But this is a question around what the global entails—i.e., what relation we are to have with global others—that requires a great deal more nuanced thought and discussion. At the very least, as this decolonial turn passes from obscurity into maturity, we need forms of design thinking and making that can negotiate between claims of decolonisation that emphasize the incommensurably different with the realities of living in an increasingly cosmopolitan, hyper-connected world also defined by continuous exchange, flow, and flux by ever renewing hybrid forms and subjects, where the boundaries between cultures cannot be neatly drawn and defined. We need thought that has the capacity to imagine and capture the immensity of the world. And for this, we need to start paying more attention to what is actually going on in the world around us.

Jun 2023
Losing the Long War
In an earlier version of this essay written on my trips in 2021, while Imran Khan was still prime minister in Pakistan, I had tried to illustrate the ways in which his political regime was deploying arguments that have interesting parallels in leftist discourses around decolonisation in the West: namely, the stress on absolute "cultural" incommensurability, epistemological decolonisation and delinking, and the reclamation of a "Pakistani" identity untethered to foreign conceptions and interests. At the same time, that language was also being fed into the projects of left-leaning pro-

gressive movements along lines that more clearly resemble the imperatives to call out Western imperialism, while at the same time stressing the importance of building local movements grounded in local knowledge.

Therefore, at the time, my perspective was squarely focused on the problem of how the conceptual vocabulary of decolonisation and decoloniality was making its way through global circuits and being deployed in different ways by both the political left and right to support different ideological and political agendas. I had argued that designers needed to pay closer attention to how the categories and concepts they used worked differently in different contexts and as parts of different projects around the world. Ironically, at a time when there has been much interest in the "local" in and through the discourse of decoloniality, the task was to develop a more "global" perspective.

Since then, much has changed in Pakistan; 2022 was a very hard year for Pakistanis. Imran Khan was ousted from power and his party dismantled by an alliance between the opposition parties and the military. Massive floods in September devastated local agriculture, displaced around thirty million people, and tipped an already shabby economy into crisis. Political instability and climate catastrophe had the added effect of tanking the economy. When I visited again in summer of 2023, inflation was at 29%, a little down from a high of 37% in May. Pakistan has just recently had its twenty-third bailout by the IMF approved (as of the summer of 2023), and, as is always the case with the IMF, this has been a Faustian deal accompanied by conditions to adopt even more austerity and injunctions to show even more growth (economics trumps any concern for welfare). This time, the intertwined twin specters of nature and economy cast a long shadow over my trip: dealing with the climate and talk of the climate was constant and could not be disentangled by talk of the economy, which is also shaped by the realities of socio-economic inequities.

The overwhelming heat and humidity in Karachi force the middle and upper classes to resort to air conditioning even as electricity bills skyrocket. What distinguishes the elite from the middle class in Pakistan is how many rooms and how often air-conditioning can be run: the former can afford to run multiple ACs all day and live in immunological bubbles isolated from the rest of the city, while middle-class families languish together in a single room during the day and turn the air conditioner off and on as the ambient temperature waxes and wanes. One used to hear about the issue of power and how wealthy families could afford fossil-fuel-powered generators large enough to run through the seven-to-eight-hour power outages in the city during the summers and monsoon season—this time, the conversations around power revolved not around the availability of power, but its expense: what distinguishes the former from the latter now is the conversion to solar power and being able to afford the upfront costs of installing solar paneling and running houses entirely off the grid.

On the plane to Karachi, I read a few essays by local journalists and climate activists on how nonexistent or unregulated development—cutting down green cover to make way for yet more high-rises and tarmac—had turned vast swathes of the city into a heat trap. Clearly the Pakistani state has done little to nothing to prepare for climate change, much less address long-standing issues of social and economic justice. No wonder then that many Pakistanis, working class and bourgeois, desperately want to leave: such was the prevailing sentiment among the few friends and colleagues I have left in the country. Yet migration too is fraught with challenges, as was made clear in the way the fate of the hundreds of Pakistani refugees was determined by the Greek coastguard and the apathetic European response to the disaster earlier in June.[1] Clearly, despite the rhetoric of justice, many lives still do not matter in the present world-system. They do matter, though, where

Editors note: On June 14th, the fishing trawler *Adriana* capsized and sank. Out of the estimated 650–750 passengers on board, only 104 were rescued. 209 passengers from Pakistan were unaccounted for and presumed dead.

Ahmed Ansari

capital is concerned, as the international search for a lost submersible with a Pakistani billionaire and his son showed us. Clearly the elite of Pakistan, as everywhere else, play by different rules.

Frantz Fanon rightly observed that the colonial world was marked by violence: not an intermittent, reactive violence— which is normally what we think of when we think of the violence of decolonisation, of movements, and of revolutions (which, as critics of Western readers of Fanon have pointed out, is a misinterpretation of his work)—but a normative, everyday violence that seeps into the fabric of life and continuously shapes its constituents. I wonder if one can make a similar assessment of postcolonial violence. After all, apart from the indirect but pervasive and continuing influence of the Anglo-Eurocentric hierarchies that structure the modern world-system (and which Latin American decolonial thought largely focuses on), the postcolonial citizen experiences violence every day from both the apathy of the state to provide the necessary conditions for life and the kind of general cruelty one finds in individuals, institutions, systems, and practices irrespective of affiliation yet specific in its relation to the particularities of the society and culture of a community and its history. What modern institutions like the nation-state, military, international and local corporations, NGOs, political and social elites, and the intelligentsia have in common is their collective capacity to monopolize the mandate for violence—this is one of the key insights of decolonial theory—yet how they do this and what forms it takes vary greatly from context to context, raising the question of whether one can use the same frames to analyze power from one to the other at all.

Fanon helps me observe the skeins of power flowing in the many tributaries and channels through everyday life. But Fanon in Karachi also frustrates me. His characterization of decolonisation as a general, focused, and decisive response to ending the writ of the ruling class chal-lenges the light of places where life still goes by, and in fact, is capable of creating and exhibiting deep beauty, despite everyday violence. Fanon reads internalized violence as eventually reaching an apex, upon which it bursts forth and sweeps away the order that created it. For this to happen there has to be a recognition of the stark difference between the order of the colonizer and that of the colonized: the world of the colonizer and colonized are intertwined but separate and compartmentalized. Yet this is not Karachi. From time to time, passivity simmers and erupts into violence: a rally at Frere Hall to demand action for climate change, party ideologues getting rowdy on the streets. There are sustained movements too, especially the labor and women's movements. Despite abjection, life goes on: people go to work, raise families, make do.

If at all there were any serious aims for epistemic decolonization, US design academia should have started by interrogating its own parochiality vis-à-vis the complexities of other landscapes across the globe: that US academics continue to focus on concepts, categories, narratives, and frames derived from the US' own histories and use them as generalizable to other contexts betrays an ongoing commitment to US (and Anglocentric) exceptionalism. More troubling is that immigrant designers and international students in the North/West, as well as local ones in the South/East, continue to find US-centric vocabularies useful ← (myth of) neutrality and utilize them unproblematically—it is particularly disheartening to see students in the US show projects that continue to reify tired old tropes since this indicates that design faculty in the US are not doing the work of getting international students to critically interrogate their own subject positions and home contexts. I might add that while this is disheartening to see, it is not surprising: design students who receive the same kind of uncritical education at home and fail to develop the skills to critically examine themselves in their own societies often peddle the same shibboleths

73

Cosmopolitanism and Difference...

when they move abroad and establish careers for themselves in other parts of the world. In many cases, I have found students who are aware of these failures in their undergraduate education, and who are further disappointed in their expectations of graduate studies in the US or Europe. This needs to change. Rather than relying on assumed definitions and easily digestible and digested platitudes, design teachers and scholars should be opening up concepts and contexts as sites for rigorous investigation.

threshold of design →

I often get asked what epistemic decolonisation might lead to in terms of a new design praxis. My answer to this is that at its heart, the project of decentering US- and EU-centric conceptions of design has to start with opening up the question of what design is. Clearly, as even a cursory assessment of sociotechnical milieus in Pakistan indicates, it is not the same activity or output there as in the United States. If we are truly committed to a politics of pluriversality, then understanding different contexts in their totality and complexity becomes a central task in being able to articulate "many designs," if we can call what happens in each context "design" at all. What do services mean in a society where servant labor is taken for granted? What does production mean in a society where most of it happens either informally or in shadow economies? How

speculation →

might we think of sustainability in a country where catastrophic climate change is not speculation but imminent reality, and where public infrastructure to cope with the latter is nonexistent and unlikely to be built?

These are questions that Pakistani students at home and abroad should be asking and investigating, and, as has been made evident during my visits in conversations with them over the last few years, many of them do recognize these questions as being important ones and want to work on them. Yet design education neither here nor there does a good job of supporting them in opening these questions up as sites of inquiry, let alone supporting their investigation. Both in Pakistan and in the United States, design education remains hopelessly parochial rather than expansive and cosmopolitan, and this needs to change.

Wait! The design studio instructor will cry (and almost always does): I'm not an anthropologist, an economist, a philosopher, or a historian! Why must opening up concepts and questions be my work! But, to paraphrase the Brazilian political philosopher Roberto Unger, to understand a phenomenon is to grasp what it can become—to speculate and imagine based on insights made possible only through scalar movements between the deep and the extensive, the local and the global. Without this kind of understanding all designers are capable of, we will see the perpetual reproduction of the present and actualize only what is already conceivable. This is where the still very fledgling disciplines of design studies and design history, which themselves are in dire need of radical transformation, might come to be useful if integrated well with a studio design curriculum.

This speaks in particular to two audiences: designers from the Global South/East in the North/West, who almost always represent the former in the latter and whose discourses and framings are often accepted unproblematically by Anglo-Europeans; and designers in the South/East, who often accept discursive frames from abroad—the intellectual lexicon of academics and practitioners in the US and Europe—without interrogating them in the light of a rigorous study of their own contexts. The central argument I was trying to make in my observations from 2021—that design discourses invoking decolonisation really need to move away from broad, sweeping claims and propositions and focus more granularly on specific contexts, landscapes, and regimes—has not changed. Nor have my claims that, paradoxically, what designers in the US need is a much more global and cosmopolitan outlook, rather than a narrow intellectual parochialism.

74

Ahmed Ansari

I hope by now it is clear that coloniality, the contours of which are here investigated through the concepts of authenticity and hybridity, nationalism and cosmopolitanism, is much more complex than simple reductions to "South-North," "East-West," "Occident-Orient," "White-Brown" binaries, and that it is also not just an epistemological phenomenon, but very much a material and praxical one: epistemological dimensions cannot be discussed without reference to material ones. This indicates that purely academic endeavors cannot work without a commitment from academics to develop critically informed forms of praxis and collective action. It is a sad truth that academics prefer endless intellectual diversions to the very straightforward, concrete, and material struggles for the things that matter most to life. Across the city of Karachi, there are individuals and communities relentlessly combating land contractors, utility mafias, corporate cartels, the state, and military, and fighting against unplanned and unregulated

material condition of →

development and the despoiling of land and labor. Designers and design academics love to raise their stories up as case studies in "resilience," share and celebrate them as models for praxis and as evidence that we are on the path to victory, yet the sad truth is that victories are few and evanescent, and act largely as reprieves against the violent hegemony of the state. If we ever stopped to take stark account of the brutality of everyday reality in the struggles of those at its vanguard for the things that matter most—not typography or interfaces or service touchpoints, but land, world, labor, freedom—things might sober up in the field and this affective circus of false celebration might give way to harder commitments.

"We," whoever we may be, are not winning the long war. We are losing.

↖ pg. 131, 135

↖ responsibilization of design

Works Cited

Al Jazeera. 2021. "Sri Lankan factory manager lynched and set on fire in Pakistan." Al Jazeera. December 3, 2021. https://www.aljazeera.com/news/2021/12/3/sri-lankan-factory-manager-lynched-and-set-on-fire-in-pakistan.

Belmekki, Belacem. 2009. "Sir Sayyid Ahmad Khan's Framework for the Educational Uplift of the Indian Muslims during British Raj." *Anthropos* 104, no. 165–72.

Chakraborty, Dipesh. *Provincializing Europe: Postcolonial Thought and Historical Difference.* Princeton, NJ: Princeton University Press, 2000.

Dawn News Team. 2021. "PM Imran announces formation of Rehmatul-lil-Alameen Authority." Dawn.com, Dawn Group of Newspapers. October 10, 2021. https://www.dawn.com/news/1651217.

Escobar, Arturo. 2018. "Designs for the Pluriverse." In *Designs for the Pluriverse: Radical Interdependence, Autonomy, and the Making of Worlds,* 2018. Durham, NC: Duke University Press.

Fraser, Nancy, and Rahel Jaeggi. 2018. *Capitalism: A Conversation in Critical Theory.* Cambridge, UK: Polity Press.

Hall, Peter A., and David Soskice. 2001. *Varieties of Capitalism: The Institutional Foundations of Comparative Advantage.* Oxford, UK: Oxford University Press.

Hoodbhoy, Pervez. 2021. "The Mutawwa Are Coming." Dawn.com, Dawn Group of Newspapers. December 4, 2021. https://www.dawn.com/news/1661873/the-mutawwa-are-coming.

Idrees, Muhammad, and Anwar Shah. "An Empirical Analysis of Educational Inequalities in Pakistan." *Pakistan Economic and Social Review* 56, no. 2 (2018): 313–24.

Jain, Kajri. 2007. *Gods in the Bazaar: The Economies of Indian Calendar Art.* Durham, NC: Duke University Press.

Khoja-Moolji, Shenila. 2017. "Pedagogical (Re)Encounters: Enacting a Decolonial Praxis in Teacher Professional Development in Pakistan." *Comparative Education Review* 61, no. S1: S146–S170.

Ministry of Federal Education & Professional Training (website). 2018. "National Curriculum Framework Pakistan." https://www.pc.gov.pk/uploads/report/NCF.pdf.

Ministry of Federal Education & Professional Training (website). 2021. "Single National Curriculum Vision." http://www.mofept.gov.pk/ProjectDetail/MzkyNDc2MjM1Y2VjYyooZDA4LTk5OTUtNzUyNDI3ZWMzN2Rm.

Moten, Fred, and Stefano Harney. 2004. "The University and the Undercommons: Seven Theses. *Social Text* 22, no. 2 (Summer): 101–115.

Obeyesekere, Gananath. 1992. *The Apotheosis of Captain Cook: European Mythmaking in the Pacific.* Princeton, NJ: Princeton University Press.

Rahman, Tariq. 2004. *Denizens of Alien Worlds: A Study of Education, Inequality and Polarization in Pakistan.* Karachi: Oxford University Press.

Sahlins, Marshall. 1995. *How "Natives" Think: About Captain Cook, For Example.* Chicago: University of Chicago Press.

Said, Edward W. 1978. *Orientalism.* New York: Pantheon Books.

Sangwan, Saptal. 1985. "Science Education in India Under Colonial Constraints (1792–1857)." *Proceedings of the Indian History Congress* 46: 441–58.

Tahir, Izza. 2022. "Decolonizing Madrassa Reform in Pakistan." *Current Issues in Comparative Education* 24, no. 1: 61–77.

Thackara, John. 2013. "Republic of Salivation (Michael Burton and Michiko Nitta)." *Design and Violence,* Museum of Modern Art. December 19, 2013. https://www.moma.org/interactives/exhibitions/2013/designandviolence/republic-of-salivation-michael-burton-and-michiko-nitta/.

Tuck, Eve, and K. Wayne Yang. 2012. "Decolonization Is Not a Metaphor." *Decolonization: Indigeneity, Education & Society* 1, no. 1: 1–40.

Making

The Joy and Politics of Printing
Danielle Aubert and Elaine Lopez

Join Danielle Aubert and Elaine Lopez in a conversation about the joy of printing and the ways that the practice can embody political antagonism and transgression.

For Elaine, the RISO printer functions as a vehicle for a pedagogical process that encourages students to make work from a place of generosity, ease, and forgiveness. It enables the discussion about radical pedagogies, non-Western perspectives, and forms of self-care to inspire form-making and self-publishing about identity, culture, and social issues.

Danielle explores a long and rich history of radical leftists working as printers. While society's dependence on print has waned, many designers continue to see potential in owning this particular means of production. Printing combines cognitive and material labor, demands attention to craft, and can bring real pleasure to those who engage with it. What are the limits and potentials of printing as a political act?

Through examples in history and pedagogical practice, these presenters prompt us to ask: Can we discern a new kind of significance for printing?

ELAINE LOPEZ

Making to Transgress:
Risograph Printing as
the Practice of Freedom

Through my practice, I create new ways of sharing, honoring, and celebrating the stories that have been neglected for too long due to white supremacy, patriarchy, and other forms of structural oppression. I create immersive graphic design experiences that challenge people to question and expand their worldview, and this methodology models an alternative way for designers to work toward a more just society.

Pressures of School,
Ease of Riso

I'd like to consider riso printing as a graphic design experience that has the potential to help students expand their worldview and liberate themselves from some of the expectations ← expectations of and stresses that studying   schooling
graphic design currently carries.

I came to this realization because it happened to me on this very machine while I was a graduate student at RISD. It was the fall semester of my thesis year, and I was in full-blown crisis mode–an experience that current students might relate to. This· is not an exaggeration: I was weeks away from walking myself to the emergency room with a panic attack when I first learned about Riso printing. To cope with what I was dealing with, I started writing daily journal entries and letters to future students about the experiences of graduate school.

I think it's very easy to look at the amazing projects that come out of programs, but not consider the mental and physical tolls they take on students. So, I began writing to demystify some of this process. I was in that frame of mind when I made my first Riso print, which was this boulder with text isolated from its surroundings. I cried a little bit when it came out of the machine, because I couldn't believe how easy it was and how beautifully it turned out. I just put an image on the glass and out came this vibrant print.

I feel like most skills in design have huge learning curves.

Think about After Effects, ← pedagogy of chaos
coding, and Cinema 4D. But with
Riso printing, I was able to
take images that I already had
on my computer and turn them
into beautiful prints in just a
few minutes.

Boulders, Riso Printing, Materiality

These are all of the words
carved on the twenty-four boulders in Dogtown, Massachusetts.
They were put there by Roger
Babson, an eccentric billionaire
looking for a way to pay local
unemployed stone cutters during
the Great Depression. He said
of this project: "My family says
I am defacing the boulders and
disgracing the family with these
inscriptions, but the work gives
me a lot of satisfaction, from
fresh air exercise, and sunshine.
I'm really trying to write a
simple book with words carved
in stone instead of printed on
paper."

This is really interesting.
I think about the parallels of
this project a lot. This very
wealthy man was trying to give
unemployed people something
to do, and he wanted to make
something very physical, right?
He could have printed a book
with these quotes, but instead,
he chose the tedious process of
defacing the giant boulders in
this place. And his family was
not happy with him for doing
this. Then I think about how I
reflected on this work; these
rocks are currently in a place
where not many people can see
them. So, I decided to take a
photograph and return them to
paper, where more people could
see them and abstract them a
little. So, I'm taking something
from a white man, technically
a wealthy white man, and then
reimagining it. That's something.

They also reflect different
values that he held, which I
think we still hold. I like the

aesthetic,
riso →

profitability
of design →

pedagogy of
forgiveness →

horizontal;
place →

simplicity of this because it
makes us question these. Do we
still hold these values? Should
we? What do they mean?

The Riso allowed me to add
a materiality to my work that
I couldn't achieve through laser
inkjet printing. These colors
are so vivid and bright, the
prints are slightly imperfect,
and overall, they are physical
objects that can be shared, sold,
traded, and distributed to the
public.

Riso Printing in Pedagogical Practice

I quickly became obsessed with
Riso printing and wanted to
share my newfound passion with
students, so I taught a Riso
workshop the following semester
and began to fuse it with my
research on culture, identity,
and equity.

I also wanted to fold in some
of the qualities of the Riso into
the course. Like, how generous is
the Riso, right? It prints a ton
of copies very quickly. It's also
forgiving—sometimes the mistakes
that come out are actually more
beautiful than what you intended.
And it's really rewarding in
that it's so satisfying to have
tangible prints to show for your
efforts. For these reasons, I
feel that the Riso is the perfect
tool to use when making work
about challenging topics like
culture and identity, or simply
to recycle work that you've made
in another class and give it a
new life, a new streaming.

I encourage students to make
from a place of joy and self-discovery without worrying too much
about perfection.

…

The Riso became this community where students could come
and help each other print and
create a lot of work. There were
Riso prints all over the wall. It
was a space with a lot of energy,
of community. People who were

The Joy and Politics of Printing

not taking the class were taught by people who were taking the class on how to use it—how to use a Riso for their projects—and it was really exciting to see this space come to life.

On Generosity, Forgiveness, and Rewarding in the Classroom

In the class, at least when we did it in person, I encouraged students to make enough prints to give to everyone else in the class. By being in this class, you ended up with a collection of Riso prints, because you were giving and receiving prints from everybody who was there. So that was also a really important part. And I think it was so radical for students—it's interesting to think about this stuff as radical because it sounds very straightforward and very simple and direct—for students to make stuff for other people in the class for free and to give each other things and to share, to deprioritize stress or anxiety, and to make from a place of joy and experimentation, to make ugly things. That was all OK. And that was radical. I could see it in the students' demeanor in the class and they would thank me. They would say, "Wow, I'm just so stressed out all the time with other classes that I never knew that learning could be fun, or that making could just be recycling things and going against all of this stuff that we are taught as designers is not okay: you need to make fresh products for every class, it all needs to be original, and it all needs to be perfect and marketable and how's it going to look in your portfolio." We don't really talk about any of those things and yet, I think a lot of the work that comes out of this class looks wonderful in a portfolio because it doesn't have a function.

radical joy →

← expectations of schooling/ mainstream pedagogy

Some of it doesn't have a function, some of it is zines and stuff—those obviously communicate ideas, and that's great. But I think by removing some of those burdens, it actually does make students value these things, like communism and community and sharing and generosity and not being stressed out.

DANIELLE AUBERT

Danielle Aubert, *The Detroit Printing Co-op: The Politics of the Joy of Printing*, Inventory Press, 2019.

On Radical Printing

Since I published research on the Detroit Printing Co-op a couple of years ago, one of the questions that has come up for me and that has come up whenever I've talked about this with other people is how this compares to the contemporary moment. In particular, Risograph printing is one of the things that often comes up: the rise in accessibility and popularity of Risograph printing. Another question, or another area that comes up, is thinking about the internal structure of the Detroit Printing Co-op itself, how the people who were involved with it self-organized.

...

If the Detroit Printing Co-op was a radical print workshop, which I think it was, there are some questions we can ask from

Danielle Aubert and Elaine Lopez

that. What made it radical? Was it the things they printed? Was it their internal structure? Was it the movements they were a part of? And then, on the other hand, we can ask: what would a radical print shop look like today?

I definitely think there are parallels between the work of the Co-op and contemporary print workshops or ad hoc spaces that designers and artists use for printing materials. I think the work Elaine just showed kind of points in that direction, especially the activity around the printer when people are in person.

Revolution and Printing

I'm using the term radical or radical left when I talk about the Detroit Printing Co-op, but before they settled on a proper name for themselves, they called themselves "The Revolutionary Printing Co-op." As I was thinking about this talk, I realized what I'm interested in thinking through is in fact revolution. ← revolutionary What role has printing played in revolutionary activities historically and what role could it play now, in 2021?

If we start from the position that extractive capitalism is exploitative and destructive to people on the planet, we agree that we want and need things to change in major systematic ways. The big question is: How do we do that? I ask that with sincerity. How do we create a world where we can take care of each other and the planet and operate, as Marx put it, "from each according to their ability to each according to their needs"? ↖ pg.95

If we look at moments in history when progressive movements made advances, we can see that one thing they had in common is that there was some kind of a mass collective mobilization behind those advances. From the French Revolution to

the height of the labor movement in the United States to the civil rights movement, the women's liberation movement, and the Egyptian revolution of 2011, the revolutions that do manage to succeed in some way have a combination of the spark that drives people out into the streets and organizing groundwork that preceded that moment. The most revolutionary activities I have seen in my lifetime or been a part of were the Black Lives Matter demonstrations in the summer of 2020, and it was clear from the way those came about that the Movement for Black Lives that had taken off in Ferguson in 2014 laid the groundwork for the nation—a nationwide response to the murder of George Floyd in 2020.

...

To come back to the revolutionary potential of printing, I think that one way to think about it is that the more closely it can be connected to a mass movement the better, or the more revolutionary, it can be. And if there is no mass movement, time → the more it can participate in laying the groundwork for those moments when the spark does come, the more effective it can be. So, the question is: What does this look like? Especially when we're talking about printing today, at a moment when we're no longer dependent upon print media for information in the way we were fifty years ago or even a hundred years ago.

The Rise and Fall of Socialist Parties and the Rise and Fall of Printing

In his 2007 essay "Socialism: A Life-Cycle," the French philosopher Régis Debray proposed the theory of the phases of media history (Debray 2007). He says that up until 1448 we were in the *logosphere* period—the period of the invention of writing. In 1448

Gutenberg printed the Bible using movable type, so Debray marks this period starting from 1448 to 1968 as the *graphosphere*. During that period you get the book, the newspaper, the political party. He marks 1968 as the end, which also coincides with the May '68 student worker movements in Paris. Since 1968, Debray says we've been living in the *video-sphere*–the time of the image, television, and screens.

One of the things I find interesting about Debray's essay is the way he ties the rise and fall of socialist parties to the rise and fall of printing. He seems to be making some connection there. and I don't necessarily take it to mean that he's saying that socialism is dead after 1968, but I do think he has a point about the waning dominance of political parties as organizing forces. And I think it's also interesting to think about the waning dominance of print, like the role of print has changed.

Debray makes the case that the typographer and the printer play key roles in the dissemination of socialist ideas. He gives examples from the Paris Commune of 1871 and says that it was a typographer Pierre Leroux who invented the word socialism. I don't know if that's a contested thing, but it's interesting if that is in fact the case.

So, the argument that socialism depends upon, and in fact is impossible without, some kind of basic political education may be one of the reasons that leftists have always gravitated toward printing. In the late 1800s and early 1900s, many anarchists or socialists were printers, and many printers were also anarchists.

Kathy Ferguson, a political scientist at the University of Hawaii, has written about this. She says that "printers and presses were central to the physical and social reproduction of the classical anarchist movement from the Paris Commune to the Second World War." She writes that because "the technology of publishing required many skilled printers, and commercial print shops often rejected anarchist materials…printing was one of the most common occupations of anarchists" (Ferguson 2014, 391, 392.).

The Detroit Printing Co-op

The Detroit Printing Co-op existed from 1970 until 1980. It was a space in Detroit where a group of people set up printing equipment that they made available to anyone who wished to use it at no charge. They had borrowed money in order to set up initially, and then they took on paid printing jobs mostly from other leftist groups to pay off their debts. Their expenses included things like rent, utilities, and materials, but pretty much anyone who wanted to go in and print was able to.

The Co-op was not a big operation, but it had an outsized impact. They managed to print some really key texts, including the first English translation of Guy Debord's *Society of the Spectacle*. They also printed this translation of *Essays on Marxist Theory of Value* by a Russian writer, Isaak Illich Rubin, which had been banned in the Soviet Union under Stalin and was virtually impossible to get a hold of. But they printed it there and distributed it.

A Site of Production: Newspaper, Exposures, Print Shop

In 1902, Lenin wrote "What Is to Be Done?" a pamphlet in which he's trying to figure out how to build up a revolutionary movement. Fifteen years later, the Russian Revolution would take place. But at this point in 1902, the movement didn't really exist

82

Making

yet. He was trying to build it up, and he makes a case for the central role of the newspaper as a critical component for organizing revolutionary activity. For Lenin, the newspaper was key not only as a vehicle for sharing socialist ideas, it was also a site of production where printers, writers, and typesetters would come together on a collaborative project.   ← horizontal

And the content is important. He writes about the role of these things called "exposures," which were little texts about specific local incidents during which workers or people had been experiencing some form of oppression—for example, a story about a boss who wouldn't let workers take a break. He argued that   ← affective these kinds of very specific per-   connection sonal stories were more impactful than certain texts on the Marxist theory of value. It can make you really mad and motivated to take action when you read about an injustice happening to somebody else in a situation that is similar to yours. It makes your situation less alienating and it also helps make you feel like you're part of this class of people, together with them.

Fredy Perlman, *Incoherence of the Intellectual* (Black & Red: 1970) pp 72–73.

THE INTELLECTUAL AS HISTORICAL AGENCY O CHANGE

1958 - 1962

For Lenin, the newspaper was a way to help workers see that these everyday injustices—sometimes minor, sometimes major—were widespread and class-based, and this would help make people feel motivated to go into the streets or actually take action. But the other aspect is the material production of the newspaper itself. The print shop is a place where people gather to cut, fold, distribute, and print. It's a meeting place. And the act of working together on a shared project involving physical labor and physical craft brings people closer together. It brings people into conversation with one another. In this instance, it doesn't necessarily follow the logic of wage labor. For Lenin, the printing press was this key node where socialism could take root.

Leftists and Printers in Detroit

To come back to the Detroit Printing Co-op in 1970, it was absolutely a key site for the sharing and development of ideas. People who spent a lot of time there were constantly debating things, like the pros and cons of trade unionism, for instance. And they were also part of a network of other leftists and printers in Detroit.

The one that I find really interesting from the perspective of revolutionary politics is Black Star, the printing arm of the League of Revolutionary Black Workers. These were Black workers who had started organizing in the Dodge Main plant in the late 1960s because Black workers were always having to do the worst, most dangerous, lowest-paid jobs.

…

They started printing newsletters. These DRUM (Dodge Revolutionary Union Movement) newsletters were distributed at the factory gates during shift changes. In an essay titled "How a Revolutionary Counter-Mood Is Made" Jonathan Flatley writes about these new newsletters and how they helped to prepare and set the mood for workers to be ready to take action (Flatley 2012). They included stories about incidents that workers had come up against, for instance—a Black worker coming in for his shift carrying his lunch in a brown paper bag and encountering a racist guard who knocked the bag out of his hands. These types of stories were shared precisely to enrage the other workers who might be in another part of the factory and not know that that was going on. There are a lot of these newsletters, and to print these, they used the paste-up method, which was the same method used at the Co-op. They had smaller tabletop printers, but sometimes they printed things down at the Co-op, which had a big offset press.

...

Both of these sites of printing, Black Star and the Detroit Printing Co-op, were in Detroit, and they contributed to the revolutionary mood in Detroit in the '70s. The fact is that the League of Revolutionary Black Workers had built the power to completely cripple the auto industry, and they did shut down plants. The newsletters they distributed played a critical role in that.

Michael Velli, *Manual for Revolutionary Leaders* (Black & Red: 1972) pp 44-45.
Note: Michael Velli was a pseudonym used by Fredy Perlman and Lorraine Perlman.

← affective connection; material condition of Black rage

The Graphic Designer, an Emergent and Growing Category of Labor

If we follow Debray's historical designations and consider that 1968 marks the beginning of the *videosphere*, then the founding of the Detroit Printing Co-op takes place at an inopportune moment, because they founded it in 1970. I think there is something to be said for this, because by 1980 when the Co-op closed, many commercial print shops were already closing. The Co-op was really only being used regularly by Fredy Perlman and a couple of people.

Things continued to shift through the 1980s in major ways. J. Dakota Brown, who writes about graphic design and labor, has noted that several key events took place in the field of graphic design in the 1980s. In 1983, Philip Meggs published his canonical history of graphic design. In 1984, Apple released the Apple IIe, which could display color graphics. Around this time,

we also get the Apple LaserWrit-
er, which was like a home printer
or an office printer. And then
in 1986 the International Typographical Union, which was one of
the longest continuously running
unions representing typesetters, was dissolved, absorbed
into other unions. So the work
of typesetters would be done
by this emergent and growing
category of labor, the graphic
designer.

← mechanisms
of maintenance

↖ pg.133

← labor; profes-
sionalization of
design

The Radical Printer of 2021: Collectivity and Connection to Movements

Returning to the question of the
radical printer of 2021. The
question is: Where can we locate
the revolutionary potential in
printing?

I think that the first point
to take away from this is the
importance of collectivity—outside of the confines of wage,
labor, and profit, even beyond
that which is self-sustaining,
or trying to build revolutionary
mood.

← collective
action/
collectivity

Marc Fisher is a Chicago
printer. He's a stalwart presence
at art book fairs, people probably know him through Temporary
Services. But I would definitely
consider him to have a radical
practice. He's done a lot of work
around prison abolition and he's
worked with Mariam Kaba. He's
very productive and does a lot
of stuff.

He recently gave a talk at
Printed Matter and he posted
his notes on Facebook. I just
thought he gave some interesting
and extremely specific advice
about how to make a living doing
this kind of work. This kind of
gets to the point of collectivity
at a moment when people are
often working alone. He says:

"Think about your publishing family. Bookstore people
are your family. People that
organize book fairs and zine
fests are your publishing family.

time →

Other publishers are your family.
People who follow your work for
years on end are your family.
Printers and binderies are your
family. The postal workers that
know you by name and that you
know by name are your family.
The person who doesn't care if
you make the free copies at work
is your family…. Your students
are your family—particularly
once they graduate or drop out,
as long as they continue making
books and zines."

I just thought this was a
nice thing. Another concrete way
to maximize the revolutionary
potential of a printing practice
is to connect as much as possible to mass movements, or to
movements that are laying the
groundwork for mass movements.
So, you know, because all these
machines are so accessible,
printing can be really solitary.
It's possible to gain access to
the means of print production
much more easily than it was a
hundred years ago.

I think the best way to be
a revolutionary printer is to
be committed to being a revolutionary. Whatever that might
mean. And that is not an easy
task, but it's achievable, I
think. It involves finding other
leftists, socialists, radicals,
and progressives doing this work
around you. It could mean going
to meetings of groups in your
area, seeing who's organizing,
joining a union, forming a union,
forming a co-op, supporting a
strike. Maybe it's navigating the
nonprofit industrial complex and
identifying who's effective, who's
actually challenging systems
of power, and who's preventing
things from moving forward and
trying to slow things down—who's
getting in the way. Which groups
are actually confronting financial capitalism?

It takes a long time for
movements to build. It's up and
down. It's not always necessarily
building. But I believe that the

way to be a radical printer is
to embed yourself in and participate in these movements. The
closer you can get to being a
part of an organized movement
that is in direct confrontation
with entrenched power structures—
like a landlord, the police, or
a crappy boss—the better. And
then what you can do, of course,
depends on where you live.
But there are always leftists,
they're everywhere.

It could also mean reading.
I think reading groups are really
important. The users at the
Detroit Printing Co-op belonged
to reading groups. They were
always reading regularly.

And then I think it also ← craft
means leaning into your craft. ↖ pg.137
Your skills and your machines
and your workspaces. And being
ready to make them available
when and if the time comes that
people want to use them. You'll
only know if you put yourself

out there and embed yourself
in these movements. People are
probably not going to come to
you and be like, *I need to print
this stuff.* It's more like, *I'm
out here, I've got these
machines.*

You also want to be prepared ↖ pg.117
for the possibility that most
of the time, the most important
thing you can do might have
nothing to do with your craft
or with printing. But then
sometimes it will and when it
does, you have the potential for
these beautiful, transformative
moments.

Union label (bug) for used on materials printed
at the Detroit Printing Co-op.

Works Cited

Debray, Régis. 2007. "Socialism:
A Life-Cycle." *New Left Review* 46
(July-August): 5–28.
    Ferguson, Kathy E. 2014.
"Anarchist Printers and Presses:
Material Circuits of Politics."
Political Theory 42, no. 4
(August): 391–414.

Flatley, Jonathan. 2012. "How a
Revolutionary Counter-Mood Is
Made." *New Literary History* 43, no. 3
(Summer): 503–525.

Danielle Aubert and Elaine Lopez

Interview with
Danielle Aubert and Elaine Lopez

The title of the talk is derived from
Danielle's book, The Detroit Printing
Co-op: The Politics of the Joy of Printing.
What does the politics of joy mean?
Elaine talked about the joy of creation
as planting a radical seed in students,
and about the fact that work should
be joyful. What do you think about the
joy → capitalist work ethic of joy, which can
be an exploitative strategy masked as a
self-affirming demand for a labor of love
and lead to the value of fulfillment over
security (healthcare, pension, etc.)? ↖ pg.122

Mar 2023

Danielle   This is a good question. When I was trying to come up
with a title for the book, and repeating the name, it was
hard not to accidentally say "the politics AND the joy of printing,"
but I purposely wanted it to be the politics OF the joy of printing,
for precisely the reasons you raise. What are the political conse-
labor → quences of enjoying one's labor? Fredy Perlman, who was one of
the founders of the Detroit Printing Co-op, explicitly removed
himself from the wage system; he writes repeatedly about the
deadening and alienating effect of selling oneself for money. The
Co-op existed outside of "wage slavery." They organized their
labor according to a different logic than the logic of the wage system. And so, in looking at some of the early, exuberantly printed
materials that Fredy Perlman worked on, it becomes even more
poignant to think that he must have enjoyed the printing process,
especially the part that involves typesetting and organizing images on a page. If he didn't take pleasure in it, why would he have

spent so much time and energy experimenting with colors and overlays and various type treatments?

Separately from the Co-op, I think a lot about when and where to take joy in one's work. Because the thing is, if you don't take pleasure in your work, the work becomes so miserable, and you really only suffer. So while it is the case that employers—capitalist owners—exploit the notion that a "happy worker" is a better worker, it is also the case that to be unhappy in one's work—to take no joy in it—is damaging to the workers themselves.

Nov 2022

Elaine Creative professions benefit from the idea (the myth?) that this type of work is more "fun" than other professions. Stylized workspaces, lax dress codes, and quirky social activities sometimes mask the long work hours and low salaries. However, it is necessary to find joy in your profession for self-preservation. Society requires us to perform labor in exchange for compensation. While acquiring an education gives us more options about which types of labor we can choose, it is still considered labor, at the end of the day. I encourage my students to listen to which projects bring them the most joy so they can later find a job that will allow them to perform these tasks. If a student doesn't enjoy designing books, they shouldn't pursue a career in publishing. I also encourage them to find joy in their ← joy assigned task—listening to their favorite song, setting a new record for themselves, or even drinking some bubble tea can make a mundane or repetitive activity more palatable.

```
In printing co-ops and in Risograph ← horizontal;
printing classrooms, there is a shift    place
of roles: students become teachers, and
both types of spaces create a form
of "horizontal" knowledge transfer and
collective making. Since activities revolve
around the machine in a specific place,
printing and teaching become an act of
place-making. Teaching becomes a way to
```

88

build connections and relationships. How
do you take these relationships to other
teaching situations, when there isn't a
common center involved?

Elaine It is always important to build community within the
classroom, regardless of the medium taught. I do this
in many ways, but my favorite way to do this is to begin each
class by asking everyone to share one thing they are grateful for
at that moment. This activity gives us time to check in with ourselves as we enter the space and to build a sense of trust and
community over time. Students also get the opportunity to learn
about their peers and find things they have in common. Making
time for activities that allow everyone to share who they are before discussing design or critiquing work is essential.

Danielle I think with any kind of horizontal knowledge transfer
there has to be some kind of common work involved.
structure (of
collectivity) → It isn't really possible to do if there is no center. The center can
even be two people working side by side. But "doing the work"
↖ pg.125 is what builds community, what builds relationships, and what,
potentially, flattens out relationships. You don't have to do the
work physically in a shared space—it's possible to build this kind
of relationship between people working remotely. But if we've
learned anything from these isolating pandemic years, it's that
working together in a shared space is certainly better for interpersonal working relationships.

Can you talk about printing and the direct
engagement with the means of production,
where a relationship might be built with
the tool and materials, as opposed to
working at an office desk. How is a
dialogue built with tools, materials, the
space, and those around you?

Danielle   In my own experience, the machines I've had relation-
            ships with are laser printers. Sometimes they feel like
roommates or studio mates. You get to know the behaviors of
each machine, how much it can handle printing at once, how
it handles paper, when and how supplies run low. People who
spent a lot of time at the Co-op would often refer to their Harris
offset press as though it had a personality of its own, or as if it
were some kind of serene presence in the space. It commanded
respect. It was hard to use and also dangerous: it could cause
physical injury if someone's hair or sleeve got caught in its gears.
As far as the space itself, Lorraine Perlman mentioned often that
it was a dank space, without good light. But I think there was
a strong energy that people brought to it, especially in the early years, when it was understood to be a shared space that belonged to everyone. They wanted everyone to take ownership of
it and build it.

```
What, to you, is craft in historical    ← responsibilization
and contemporary design, and what are      of design; craft
its values? How are aesthetic values
affected when designers are asked to
take on additional responsibilities (such
as dismantling structures of capital and
responding to climate change)?
```

Elaine   Craft can demonstrate the amount of time and effort
          dedicated to a piece, and this can communicate care
and intention to the reader or audience. Through this lens, craft
is another vehicle for communication. However, the "lack of
craft" or medium and materials used can also communicate
urgency. Using certain materials or techniques may not be appropriate when a message needs to be disseminated rapidly. It
is crucial to consider craft and how its intended audience will
perceive it.

90

Danielle   I think of craft as the accumulation of very specific knowledge about how to cause material to transform in a particular way, if that makes sense. As a graphic designer, if you do a lot of book design, you "hone your craft" by learning about different binding techniques, hot glue, cold glue, when and how to do a face trim, paper grain orientation, paper type, how to design a page in such a way that it will produce one effect craft → or another when printed. So, I guess craft is not exclusively connected to manual production, like the act of printing. It seems to me that one can engage with craft in various ways—it just means knowing your material. I once heard a union organizer say to another union organizer that they admired that person's craft. By which I think they meant that organizer's ability to navigate conversations and, essentially, radicalize people to care about their working conditions enough to join their union. I suppose I don't think of craft as exclusively a time-consuming thing. It just means knowing your material and knowing how to account for various

↖ pg.137 external conditions. Craft is something that is learned over time.

Physical, printed artifacts often get
digitized and circulated as digital
artifacts in portfolios, talks, promotions
in online shops, etc. The circulation of
digitization creates a larger collective
understanding, but what's lost in the
process? What is the significance of
digitization and the different experience
it creates?

Elaine   The digitization of printed artifacts can occasionally lead to deception, especially regarding the sale of printed materials. I am disappointed by online purchases sometimes, because the documentation leads me to expect something different than what I've received. At the same time, design is often about seduction and deception, and designers are expected to use their skills to make a product appear as desirable as possible. Book fairs and stores provide an antidote to this because they allow us to experience printed materials fully before purchasing.

Danielle   I have thought about this a bit, because I decided to make a book about the materials printed at the Detroit Printing Co-op, rather than a digital archive, which would arguably have been more easily accessible. One obvious difference between a digital online archive and a printed book is that a book is a fixed container, and it allows space for creating a narrative. I think it's harder for digital archives to provide consistent space for a narrative—for writing about the contents of the collection. More people can see the images, but we may not know what we're looking at.

Elaine, You emphasized the act of printing over content, process over product. In this process, it is through making that reflexive thinking that is responsive to what's printed can be learned. Tacit knowledge is translated through doing, artifacts serve as the evidence of learning. Can you elaborate on your pedagogy along these lines? Is the tool taking over the creation? How much do you control with the tool?

Elaine   While the Riso can be easy to use, it certainly requires mastery of the pre-press processes to achieve intended outputs. It is through an understanding of these processes—overprinting, color theory, registration, and cropping—that successful prints are produced. In this case, the tool has implications for what you can create—but this applies to most design software and hardware. These restrictions give students some ← pedagogy of chaos parameters that help narrow down the possibilities of what to make. Some specific limitations in Riso printing include the weight, texture, and size of the paper that can be printed on, the particular colors you have access to, and the misregistration that

92

is likely to occur from print to print. These factors will undoubtedly influence what is produced, but that is part of the fun.

> Your pedagogical ethics of generosity and
> forgiveness, encouraging the reuse and
> recycling of content, exist in contrast
> to the pressure of originality expected
> by institutions and the hyper-productivity
> expected in the context of neoliberal
> working conditions. How does this
> translate when students enter the labor
> force with less forgiveness and deadlines?
> How could we expand this ideal outside of
> work and the bubble of a class/semester?

Elaine It is unrealistic to expect perfection and mastery from students learning a skill. Much of the anxiety and depression my students experience comes from the high expectations set early on in their education. The classroom should be a space of exploration, trial and error, and growth. How can we expect originality and creativity if students never get the opportunity to experiment? Hyper-productivity results in the proliferation of the same generic aesthetics that lead to unoriginal portfolios. Students need the time and space to play, so they know what it feels like to produce from a place of joy. I hope they will carry this experience into the workforce and advocate for change and humane working conditions that allow them to be genuinely creative.

> Danielle, Do you see the rising number of
> co-ops as a nostalgic evolution, or as a
> way to seek out new possibilities? What
> are the potentials and pitfalls of the co-
> op as a form for organizing design labor?

Danielle I don't think the co-op form is nostalgic. Maybe they're not as common as they should be, because there is too much pressure to organize hierarchical structures. But it makes sense as a way for a group of individuals to organize themselves.

I think the situation is rather that it can be hard to do. There are external, financial pressures that make it hard for a group to stay non-hierarchical. Sometimes it might just be easier to have a couple of people be "in charge" and then hire contractors. But when I think of craft co-ops or housing co-ops... I know of co-ops that are long-lasting, and I think one characteristic is that they settled into pretty clear organizational patterns over time. For instance, they might end up electing a "president" from among their members, or someone to be in charge for a designated amount of time. They might follow Robert's Rules of Order during meetings, or some other clearly understood method for organizing decision making. They probably end up with bylaws of some kind. I think it can be nearly impossible for co-ops to survive when the structure is completely horizontal and there are no rules.

> How do your research on the printing
> co-op and your organizing influence or
> become integrated into your pedagogy? How
> would you orient students towards co-ops
> as a form of organizing?

Danielle   I cannot say that I've oriented my students toward the co-op model. I work with undergraduates, and usually their first employment after school is working for someone else, or freelancing. So, I haven't had many opportunities to talk to them about forming co-ops. If they were to form co-ops it would most likely be several years after graduation—after they'd been through other modes of employment. But I think organizing has worked its way into my teaching more around the idea of self-determination. Encouraging students to define what they want, ← collective action/ collectivi
force change, and not wait to be "given" power.

    After the school shooting at Michigan State University this winter, my students came to class extremely angry—about the shooting, about inaction on the part of legislators to stop it,

Danielle Aubert and Elaine Lopez

about having had to come to school the day after the shooting and pretend like everything was normal. Many of them remembered the Oxford High School shooting that took place just a year ago. Many of them knew students at MSU or knew students who went to high school with the victims. In that conversation, I was a bit at a loss, but then weirdly, I suggested they join the Student Senate, which is not something I would have thought of myself as recommending. I happened to know that the Student Senate, as a body, has a lot of power with administrators on campus. It's also a body that art and design students have very little to do with—there is rarely any representation from our college. Recently, the Student Senate has been debating politically charged issues like support for Palestine and pressuring the university to divest from Israel. They have sent representatives to meetings of the campus-wide Coalition of Unions, against the will of administrators, where they hear about university staff issues. It ended up being the Student Senate that organized a vigil for MSU students who died. It was also the student governance group at MSU that weighed in on when they should open the campus back up.

As I heard myself telling them to get involved with Student Senate, I thought, this was also part of getting them to engage now. Not to wait. Something other than the guidance to "write to your state legislator." We can talk about organizing co-ops or taking action at some later date, but they're students *now*, they're in Detroit *now*, things are happening *now*, and as students I want them to recognize the levers of power in front of them.

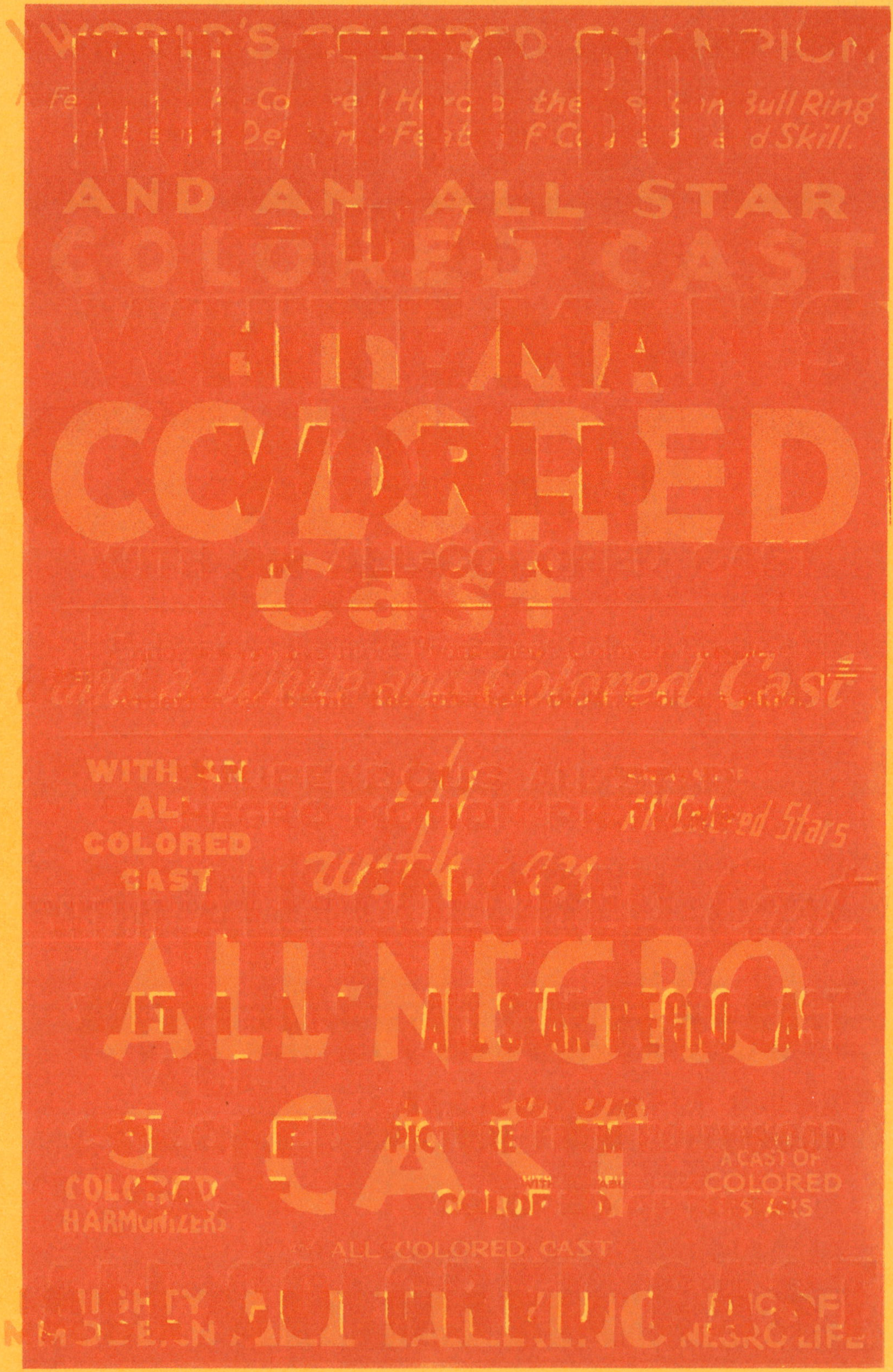

Kelly Walters. An All Colored Cast No3.

Remixing Design
as a Radical Act

Kelly Walters

When I was growing up, my Dad would play vinyl records on his stereo system on the weekends. He would turn the volume all the way up so it could make its way from the basement to our bedrooms on the second floor. It was his "subtle" way of waking up me and my brothers so that we could begin our weekend chores (cleaning our rooms, helping with the laundry). Some weekends I'd hear The Temptations, others it might be Chaka Khan or Bob Marley. I vividly remember looking at the cover design for Michael Jackson's *BAD* album when I was about nine or ten, sifting through the records in his collection. Not really knowing anything about typography or what graphic design was at this point, I was drawn to the way text and imagery were paired. I also didn't quite have the vocabulary to describe why I liked the way the uppercase black letters sat beneath the word *BAD* spray painted in bright red. Alongside that was this very focused image of Michael Jackson in his black leather jacket. These aspects—the type, the photograph, and the fashion felt cool to me (or at least, cool by '90s standards). The more I rifled through my Dad's records, the more I began to think about the ways other popular Black performers were being styled and packaged for a 12" × 12" square.

** Today, when I look through archives, I am always interested in what the design work says, what it conveys, and what its original function once was. I see this as a pedagogical practice that is directly informed by close looking. The skill of looking closely was fostered and nurtured during my time as an art and design student. My professors would encourage us to observe any and all visual details because they could eventually become inspiration for one's design project. I learned quickly that small details could be isolated, extracted, or transformed into new forms. When I was a graduate student, I produced one project that embodied this process: *Hidden Beauty* (2015). The project brief included finding an object in the RISD Museum that could serve as inspiration for a folded broadsheet poster. Initially, I was disappointed by the lack of Black representation in the collection as I moved through the museum; I could not "see" myself among the various European paintings. It wasn't until I came across two sculptures, Charles Cordier's *African Venus* (ca. 1851) and Joseph Chinard's Bust of Madame Récamier (after 1801) that I felt something click. What was significant was that these two sculptures were both commentaries on Black and white conceptions of beauty. I photographed each sculpture to capture its surface textures, variations in hairstyle, and facial expressions. The folded broadsheet poster enabled me to hide and reveal sections of these photographs and written text I emphasized for the viewer.

material
condition of
representation
and erasure →

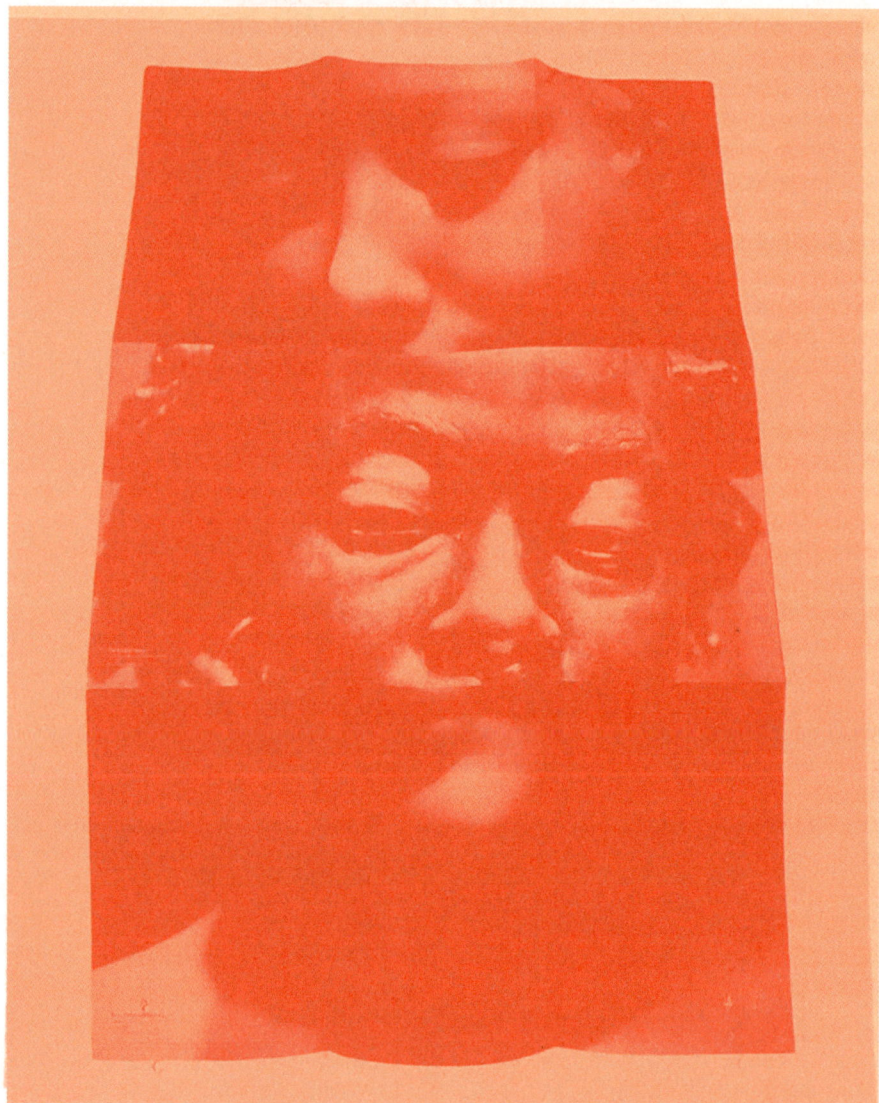

Kelly Walters, *Hidden Beauty*, 2015.

Kelly Walters

Ultimately, this poster was both a critique of the museum collection and a way for me to reflect on Black female representation. In my MFA thesis book, *Sitcoms, Slow Jamz & The White Cube*, I share deeper reflections on this project. "In questioning the physical characteristics that made them 'elegant,' 'pure' or 'real,' Hidden Beauty began to highlight these late 19th-century notions of exoticism and beauty...." (Walters 2015) Establishing a critique that can provide new meaning or act as an educational entry point is the reason I design. Activating racial stereotypes found in museum collections or archives provides an opportunity for new questions that confront the past to emerge. Questions like: How have Black images been shaped through ← projection the lens of whiteness? How do archives perpetuate and maintain ra- ← mechanism of maintenance cial tropes and stereotypes? How can design be used to create counternarratives that disrupt demeaning depictions?

material condition of representation and erasure →

↖ pg. 50,57

Cut to years later, in July 2018: I was attending an artist' residency in Los Angeles. It is here that I would continue to explore these themes in a more expanded way. During my time in the city, I visited the Margaret Herrick Library at the Academy of Motion Picture Arts and Sciences and the USC Cinematic Arts Library. I looked through several photographs, books, and archival documents related to the evolution of Black popular entertainment in the United States. The promotional materials in their collections showcased the shifts from stereotypical depictions of Black performers to imagery that aspired to be more authentic in its portrayals. These collections also demonstrated that language played an important role in racial transformation, particularly as it was concerned with how Black people had been historically "labeled" in American culture.

I think of my practice as sitting at the intersection of this evolution of "racial labeling" and how print material from Black entertainment (i.e., leaflets, playbills, and promotional signage) could embody these changes within its art direction. Understanding the history of terms ← projection such as "negro" as it transitioned to "Black" and "African American" is important in the context of the design canon. In *Changing Racial Labels*, Tom W. Smith describes the evolution of the terminology used to describe Black Americans, explaining that, "While many different racial terms have been used throughout their history, the standard preferential term changed from 'Colored' in the nineteenth century and early twentieth century to 'Negro' from then until the late 1960s, then to 'Black,' and now perhaps to 'African American.' While the preferred term has changed several times, the common goal for Blacks has been to find a group label that instilled group pride and self-esteem" (Smith 1992, 497). These racial identifiers appear in graphic ← material condition of representation and erasure design artifacts (as type choice, image style, AAVE vernacular) and reflect the ways in which Black people have been pigeonholed, or, conversely, began to assert greater authority over how they chose to be identified.

*
** As with the *BAD* album I encountered as a kid, I kept coming back to images of Blaxploitation film posters. I was struck by the bold letterforms. A few specific film posters—those for *Super Fly* (dir. Gordon

Parks, Jr., 1972), *The Mack* (dir. Michael Campus, 1973), *Foxy Brown* (dir. Jack Hill, 1974), and *Shaft* (dir. Gordon Parks, 1971)—all embodied a typographic dimensionality in their title marks. From the superfluous curves and deep drop shadow of *Super Fly* to the extended swashes of *Foxy Brown*, these letterforms were meant to project power. I immediately started scanning and cropping fragments of these film titles once I got back into the studio. I was also fascinated by the subheadings used to describe Black performers and productions. For some of the earlier twentieth-century print material, I generally pulled the text that felt jarring and racially problematic, such as "with a cast of colored stars" or "stupendous all-star negro motion picture." These phrases were reflective of the Jim Crow era and framed segregation in the margins of the design. With all these various text fragments stretching across time, I created a series of digital patterns and collages. In many of the patterns, I tried to isolate sections of text to make it more obscure, while in other instances, I tried to focus on its most recognizable shapes. Eventually, I used risograph and silkscreen printing to output my designs. The combination of these mediums allowed me to work with different tactile surfaces such as paper and fabric and create a variety of textual experiments.

I believe 1970s visual material became significant to my process because it was emblematic of the era when my parents were coming of age. This passing down and re-sharing of musical genres like funk, soul, hip-hop and R&B are so present in Black American culture. Numerous hip-hop songs have been sampled from earlier Black performers and musical genres. A few notable ones permanently imprinted in my mind are The Sugarhill Gang's "Rapper's Delight" sampled from Chic's "Good Times" and The Notorious B.I.G.'s "Juicy" sampled from Mtume's "Juicy Fruit." These songs are classics and hold so

time; place → much meaning across multiple generations in the Black and African American communities. For me, just hearing the first three bars of any of these songs situates me in a Black space, place, and time.

I'm interested in how a snippet can be recognized.

Similarly to a hip-hop artist, I visually sample by culling these fragments of text and/or image. By pulling from multiple sources like the *Super Fly* or *Shaft* posters and transforming them into new works, a new space for dialogue with an earlier form opened up. Writer Tom Perchard explores the concept of digital sampling and the ways in which it can be "traced" within and across Black musical genres in his essay, "Hip Hop Samples Jazz: Dynamics of Cultural Memory and Musical Tradition in the African American 1990s." Perchard builds his argument based on two key music theorists who explain the influence and impact of sampling (Perchard, 2011). The first is Russell A. Potter who notes, in his book *Spectacular Vernaculars: Hip-Hop and the Politics of Postmodernism*, that, "hip-hop's continual citation of the sonic and verbal archives of rhythm and blues, jazz, and funk forms and re-forms the traditions it draws upon" (Potter 1995, 26). The second theorist is Kyra D. Gaunt, who articulates that hip-hop sampling is, "the perfect medium for expressing the temporal culture-scape of who

100

we are, and how we became, across time" (Gaunt 1995, 118). These theoretical outlooks (both unconscious and fully aware) let me be in communion with Black material culture. I liken my process to that of musical sampling because, in many ways, the idea of freestyling and remixing feels like a radical act. One definition of *radical* can be defined as being, "of or going to the root or origin; fundamental." For me, working with the "root" is key to understanding.

reassembling →
↖ pg.48,56

** Beyond sampling from archival material, thinking through these themes in a curatorial context has also created additional spaces to explore the legacy of Black representation. In January 2022, I curated an exhibition titled *With a Cast of Colored Stars* for the Aronson Gallery at Parsons School of Design in New York. The exhibition included work across a variety of mediums—zines, posters, video, patterns, and photography—that drew inspiration from Black film posters and music sheet covers from the 1920s through to the 1970s. The curatorial approach aimed to feature promotional material from early Black cinema and music. One critical text guiding my research was John Duke Kisch's *Separate Cinema: The First 100 Years of Black Poster Art* (1992). I came across this book during my residency in Los Angeles and it was the first time I encountered a book dedicated to Black film posters. The range of Black representations it features became an anchor for the exhibition and led me to look into other archives such as those housed at the National Museum of African American History and Culture or the New York Public Library Digital Collection. These archives' digital collections provided access to additional film-related material like lobby cards from the film *Flying Aces* and music sheet covers featuring Blackface performers like Al Jolson. I was excited to share a few reproductions of these works in the exhibition because they focused on the evolution of Black culture in the realms of theater, film, and music.

The show was arranged into four thematic sections. The first featured an image grid of Black film posters (On Stage), music posters from the Globe Collection and Press at MICA (Band & Show), and a collection of vinyl record covers (Live). The second thematic section featured reproductions of theater posters, music sheet covers, and film lobby cards from the early to mid-twentieth century. These images were placed on the wall chronologically to demonstrate the progression of image style and language treatment influenced by race. The third section featured original work by artists and designers who *re-interpreted*, *re-envisioned*, and *re-mixed* visual representations from these historical artifacts. Finally, the fourth thematic section included work produced by Parsons School of Design students from my "Black Visual Culture" class. My students were encouraged to develop work that experimented with imagery, typography, color, and pattern using digital and analog printmaking processes.

Given the limited access to the show due to the university's pandemic restrictions, most visitors to the exhibition were members of The New School community. Despite this constraint, I organized gallery tours for Communication Design, Fine Arts, and Illustration students.

Creating opportunities for students to ask questions and draw their own connections allowed us to think through the various perspectives shown in the work. Some of the questions that surfaced included: What images and styles are recurring? What languages are being used (i.e., slang, code-switching)? How can sound be used to reinforce aspects of representation? How do we emphasize or speculate on our understanding of Black identities? These tours were eye-opening because I learned that many students and faculty felt there had never been a show quite like that held in the Aronson Gallery before. Some faculty also shared that it was one of the most engaging exhibitions because there was so much visual material to explore and analyze. *With a Cast of Colored Stars* demonstrates one way to invite students to hold critical discussions about how art and design forms can address questions of race.

← speculation/ imagination

** When I think about my working design methodologies and the curation of *With a Cast of Colored Stars*, I see a collective practice that supports the excavation of design history. Whether I am working independently or in collaboration with other artists, I have a deep commitment to asking questions, being disruptive, and reshaping existing materials, which enables me to become a critical designer. These interactive prompts aid my deeper research and help students learn history through physical and tactile explorations. *With a Cast of Colored Stars* is an example that educators can integrate into their curricula because it builds a platform for thinking through making and critiquing existing works. This reflexive process is important in today's landscape because it helps build social consciousness and awareness of the impact of representation. It also helps situate our historical past within our present and explain why particular outlooks, tropes, or perspectives were possible in the first place. I argue that many of these designs were based on the white gaze, particularly the earlier works that include minstrel and caricature illustrations. Having the ability to interpret and interrogate archival design forms is a necessary skill in the classroom and beyond, as a professional designer. These are also radical acts that we must implement every day in order to push beyond the implicit and explicit bias in the making of design.

← material condition of representation and erasure ↖ pg.56

Works Cited

Gaunt, Kyra D. 1995. "The Veneration of James Brown and George Clinton in Hip-Hop Music: Is It Live! Or Is It Re-memory?" *In Popular Music: Style and Identity*, edited by Will Straw, 117–22. Montreal: Centre for Research on Canadian Industries and Institutions.

Perchard, Tom. 2011. "Hip Hop Samples Jazz: Dynamics of Cultural Memory and Musical Tradition in the African American 1990s." *American Music* 29, no. 3 (Fall): 277–307.

Potter, Russell A. 1995. *Spectacular Vernaculars: Hip-Hop and the Politics of Postmodernism*. Albany: State University of New York Press.

Smith, Tom W. 1992. "Changing Racial Labels: From 'Colored' to 'Negro' to 'Black' to 'African American.'" *The Public Opinion Quarterly* 56, no. 4 (Winter): 496–514.

Walters, Kelly. 2015. "Sitcoms, Slow Jamz & The White Cube." MFA thesis, Rhode Island School of Design.

On the Performative Commitment to Decolonisation Within Liberal Design Education

Hayfaa Chalabi and Maya Ober

This text is neither neutral nor objective. Drawing on feminist traditions that lend importance to everyday life as socio-political configurations (Katz 1996), we share our lived experiences of institutional life in the particular territory of Western European design schools. Our writing "does not claim to produce an objective or truthful account of reality" (Pink 2007, 22). Instead, we use ethnographic snippets as a creative way of representing our insights on design education from within our multiple experiences (ibid). Some stories were brought to us by the students whom we have been listening to, trying to be attuned to those who are tuned out (Ahmed 2021). Some we witnessed directly. They all express frustration, which, to echo Sara Ahmed, serves as a feminist record of our attempts, struggles, and failures.

October 2021. We are visiting the graduate show of a prestigious design school in the Netherlands. A wall covered with numerous black-and-white signs catches our attention. The cover of a Quran is reproduced on one of the signs and turned upside down, with the book's spine on the left side. As Arabic readers—native and non-native—we immediately notice the extremely odd mistake—Arabic is read right-to-left, and books are usually bound on the right side. We approach the freshly graduated MA student and ask them about it. They hadn't seen the error, nor had several tutors and students engaged with the project over the past semester. The work laments, as the student claims, the "post-ISIS contamination of Iraq," but it preserves US-American and imperialist "innocence" despite the primary responsibility of these for the devastation of the region of Hayfaa, where one of the authors of this text is from.

Similarly problematic scenes are too often repeat. One student designed what they named a "Japanese" ceramic tool, claiming that its minimalist and organic form derives from the island's culture, thus reinforcing the widespread practice of appropriating and fetishizing Japanese aesthetics in industrial design. Yet their presentation could have done more to demonstrate if and how they engaged with Japanese

105

design to address their own positionality as a white designer and tackle the issues of cultural appropriation.

Another presents research on the representation of Egyptian women in photography but is unreflexive about the white gaze their work enacts. Yet another student explores an Indigenous notion of design in Latin America and claims that their method is informed by animism, while another wants to build "dialogue" between Swiss design and Ghanian craft but overlooks the power imbalance of the involved parties. One can't help but think of colonialism and its extractive relationship with cultures, practices, and lifeways rooted in places far from the imperial metropoles. Every semester we are confronted with well-intentioned student projects that seek to engage with pressing contemporary social and environmental justice struggles, explore cross-cultural collaborations, and expand the understanding of design beyond its horizons of problem-solving and service provision. Students rarely take into account their respective positionalities in relation to the subject matter. Their works often lack a critical reflection on their "design politics," a term elaborated by design researcher and anthropologist Mahmoud Keshavarz to emphasize the interconnectedness of these two fields of knowledge (Keshavarz 2020).

mechanisms of maintenance →

promise of design schools →

Back at the exhibition, we talk to the student, asking whether they received the necessary support from the department or a tutor who has knowledge of their research matter. Their categorical "no" was unsurprising. Many design programs across Europe have started promoting themselves as intellectual sanctuaries wherein students can explore questions of decolonization and foster engagements with feminist and Indigenous practices and knowledges. Regretfully, the promise of facilitating such work often remains just that, because the teaching staff lack the tools, knowledge, resources, time, and sometimes the will to engage meaningfully with, say, depatriarchalizing and decolonizing their educational programs. It is in this context that the Decolonising Design collective advises us that opposing the status quo would entail "delivering the kinds of knowledge and understanding that are adequate to addressing long-standing systemic issues of power" (Decolonising Design 2016). Consequently, students who desire a critical, oppositional framework for their education are left largely to their own devices and sent on an impossible mission to attain it. The institution expects students and faculty to tackle critical social and political issues yet fails to supply the requisite support. This may be one reason that, despite all good intentions, we continue to see the reproduction in students' work of the white, colonial gaze and the perpetuation of its hegemony. This is particularly evident in the persistence of heteronormative, able-bodied cis-male subjects as the universal "user," as well as the retention of normative assumptions about form reinforced by a European and North American design canon set as the standard against which the formal tendencies of other people and cultures are measured.

In this context, students of color, migrants, womxn, and others from marginalized backgrounds find themselves isolated and misunderstood. Oftentimes, their work tries to critically engage with dominant norms and power structures based on their lived experiences, but is labeled as irrelevant in schools that insist on the fantasy of apolitical design education and practice. Students dealing with reactionary design-political boundaries have shared with us feelings of isolation, abandonment, and loneliness in their studies and practice. When predominantly white, hetero-patriarchal institutions are challenged to "decolonize," it is often marginalized students who are burdened with providing solutions to design schools and the oppressive legacy of design in curricula.

← labor
↖ pg. 71,119

One would not be surprised to hear faculty saying, both officially and unofficially:

"We have asked the students to include this 'decolonization' in their research."

"The students will suggest books to decolonize our reading list."

"We couldn't find any female and non-Western authors, so we asked the students to share some with us."

We hear such statements regularly in our educational practices in Switzerland and the Netherlands. The onus for transforming design education and practice towards a more critical and equitable one lies on the shoulders of student-led initiatives or activist teachers.

As a female Iraqi Swedish immigrant living in Holland and a female Ashkenazi Jewish immigrant based in Switzerland, we try to support these alienated students with care and compassion, drawing on our own lived experiences of exclusion and discrimination. However, we often fail. The work this entails comes to us as a burden, but it is necessary to take up. Or, perhaps it is a necessary burden. In any case, we are situated at an impasse, which has generated a commitment that also prompts us to ask ourselves if it is futile.   ← care work

"Queer and feminist worlds are built through the effort to support those who are not supported because of who they are, what they want, what they do."
(Ahmed 2017, 48).

Echoing feminist scholar Sara Ahmed's words, our will is to create networks of support and to strive toward design education *otherwise,* a practice that is critical, situated, reflexive, and socially transformative (Abdulla 2018). We want to continue to build feminist worlds.

Over the years, we have been invited to give workshops and talks or to participate as guests in different design schools to share our critical view of design as a situated practice that inherently creates and reinforces social hierarchies. Many students have approached us seeking guidance, a "feminist ear" for their grievances, or, most importantly, for solidarity (Ahmed 2021). We are often, unfortunately, in a precarious situation, invited for a very brief period of time to an institution and unable to consistently engage or even attempt the induction of structural and curricular changes.

Our encounters in these scenarios demonstrate repetitive patterns: a final-year student wishing to explore a socio-political topic with a supervisor who is unwilling to consider any visual formal tendencies that challenge the colonial normativity of Western design; a critically conscious student stubbornly silenced by their teachers for failing to respect the boundaries of an "apolitical" discussion about visual literacy; a student of color exasperated after repeatedly looking for guidance and approval from their teachers every time words like "decolonization," "cultural appropriation," and/or "inclusive design" occur in any discussion.

Cosmetic Change

Responding to the agitation generated by the social movements of the past decade (#NiUnaMenos, #BlackLivesMatter #MeToo, and others) and student pressure to address these urgencies in the curriculum— institutions strive for more inclusive environments. However, it manifests as performative inclusivity—a band-aid on an open wound unsuccessful in its attempts to respond to intensifying student demands for higher education models that counter patriarchal-modernist curricular frameworks.

Instead of a deeper, critical engagement with Western canons, the underpinning sociopolitics of the human-made world, and the complicity of academic institutions in upholding colonial and patriarchal epistemologies, design schools prefer more cosmetic changes. "Inclusivity," for instance, has become a buzzword in Western design institutions. Its mobilization echoes the way that the British Empire "included" colonized subjects in its colonial administration. Design schools fall into the trap of tokenism in hiring practices, following an additive approach to satisfy agitators' demands. However, these measures only sustain existing power structures, "offsetting demands for radical systemic change" (Decolonizing Design 2018). The result is that these faculty often find themselves isolated in their relative specialness.

`cosmetic change/` `empty gestures →` `↖ pg.65`

One problem with such forms of bureaucratic tokenism is the continuous lack of accountability in Western educational structures. Instead of accountability toward violent educational systems that privilege certain voices over others, these institutions decide to put the labor of deconstructing oppressive histories on the systemically marginalized. Colonial design curricula are overwhelmingly white systems premised upon a narrative that elevates Western, patriarchal (read: colonial) "design" above its constitutive other, "craft" (read: "vernacular," Indigenous, "ethnic," female, the so-called "rest"). This other is now made responsible by institutions for redressing an oppressive history of design that consistently marginalized them. The burden of decolonizing design curriculum through the work of "othered" subjectivities reinforces the old colonial trope wherein the oppressor's problematic burden is foisted upon the oppressed. The Western design school admonishes its included other: "If you want to save yourself, you have to save the institution too!"

`account-` `ability/` `complicity;` `labor →`

However, decolonizing design and design education cannot mean a merely additive change; rather, as the Decolonizing Design collective has proposed, it requires an ontological one. Rethinking design education from this perspective reveals the *political being* of design and its societal and environmental implications. This process of decolo-

108

nizing does not purport to create a singular new lens for design and design education, nor does it imply a simple replacement of the Western universalist model with another one (Ansari 2018; Decolonizing Design 2018; Escobar 2015). Instead, it postulates the development of multiple practices that exist in a "critical dialogue between diverse critical epistemic/ethical/political projects" (Grosfoguel 2011, 3).

It is an ongoing practice that attempts to unlearn colonial power dynamics by challenging inherited Western notions of taste and quality. The practice of decolonial design education is to be found in the ability of managers, coordinators, teachers, and students to position and question their power inside educational institutions: in critically engaging with the references and histories they discuss; in creating a horizontal learning dynamic where knowledge is expanded rather than trans- ferred; in supporting each other in the understanding that there are no shortcuts to creating a self-conscious practice capable of self-criticism; in cultivating a capacity for reflecting critically on the power structures and social hierarchies design could reproduce or disrupt.

← horizontal

Double Standards

There is often a vast discrepancy between the kind of education institutions outwardly present in their mission statements and students' lived reality once inside. In the last five years alone, we have heard of multiple encounters in which educational institutions of art and design across Europe showed works by students of color on their websites, yet those same students have told us that their teachers disapprove of their projects. Publishing such works has a promotional function, and putatively attracts applicants seeking an inclusive environment. Indeed, students struggle to work on projects that tackle themes and forms exceeding the normative expectations of professionally oriented design and design school curricula.

← normative
evaluation; promise
of design schools

This struggle can be considered through a psychological lens. US graphic designer Forest Young elaborates on Daryl Bem's psychological idea that the "exotic becomes erotic" to chart the reception of stereotypes and expectations in designed form. The theory suggests that there is a threshold at which something exotic generates a range of responses, from curiosity to arousal. However, something that is too unfamiliar might trigger fear and rejection. This idea could model the way that white teachers look at and assess works that revolve around/or are made from the standpoint of "othered" identities, subaltern themes, and unfamiliar forms. While exotic works (such as those that affirm white, cishet male expectations, and racial/gender stereotypes) may be accepted within normative educational assessments constructed around a white, cishet male worldview, the too unfamiliar will elicit confusion and punishment (Samarskaya 2022).

Making work from a marginalized standpoint and exploring formmaking that exceeds and subverts narrow, facile, and stereotypical Western expectations is fraught with risk. The student who considers doing this work risks two kinds of potential responses. Either it doesn't fit into any normative evaluative framework and is met with dismissal, derision, or worse, silence; or the work similarly makes little sense within common, normative evaluation frameworks, but the commentary is patronizing, laced with micro-aggressions, and/or met with little substantive criticism—sometimes a pitiful expression of "Oh, isn't that nice!" or "Thank you for helping me see how I have power over you. Well done." Effectively, this leaves absolutely no space for work that could disrupt default norms in design and counter colonial narratives. The disruption of the status quo is deeply related to decolonization, as educator and designer Danah Abdulla explains: "decoloniality is about *shattering* the familiar" (quoted in Khandwala 2020, our emphasis). She says that design today does not disrupt the status quo; it does not disorder the established order. Following Abdulla, decoloniality is about "reimagining something beyond the current system we exist in" (Khandwala 2020).

Performative Neutrality

It's May 2021. Diana Al-Halabi, a student and artist at the Piet Zwart Institute, hangs a Palestinian flag on the school's building in solidarity with the victims of the ongoing Israeli-led evictions in the East Jerusalem neighborhood of Sheikh Jarrah, which has been under Israeli military and administrative occupation since 1967. The residents of the neighborhood are predominantly descendants of Palestinians who were expelled from the Israeli-held West Jerusalem during the 1948 *Nakba* (the Arabic word for catastrophe), upon the creation of the settler-colonial state of Israel. The repeat eviction orders form part of a broader ethnic cleansing campaign occuring daily across Palestine.

The school removed the Palestinian flag immediately. The policing of the building intensified as security guards performed hourly patrols to check if the flag had been raised again. Al-Halabi and other students decided to hang a banner featuring a watermelon—a fruit that carries the same colors as the Palestinian flag and has become a symbol of Palestinian resistance (Anania 2021). That banner was taken down an hour later. Following weeks of confrontations between the students and the school administration, Al-Halabi designed *Holding Palestine*—a seven-day-long performance inviting students, tutors, and supporters to hold the banner with the Palestinian flag in rotation. The dean of the school invited the students involved in performing *Holding Palestine* for a conversation to discuss the reasons for removing the flags. The institution explained that the banner "carried political messages which contradicted the art school's ethics and mission" (Institutional Solidarity n.d.). However, this same school proudly and publicly condemned the 2015 shooting at the *Charlie Hebdo* office in Paris, belying its "ethics and mission" of staying out of politically charged matters (Lorusso 2021). The institution clearly applied a double standard when dealing with politics. Some events were "too political" to be addressed, while others were eagerly commented upon with a clear stance. The school's response was both exclusive and oppressive. It exposed the school's inability to take an authentic, principled political stance. It also demonstrated that what happens inside

110

the school and what happens in the world—or more specifically, anything that happens outside the Western world—are separate matters. Nevertheless, by maintaining the conceit of "neutrality," the institution in fact took a political stance against the oppressed (Barišić 2015).

Feminist Ear

Sarah Ahmed writes that, "to hear with a feminist ear is to hear who is not heard, how we are not heard" (Ahmed 2021, 4). Over the years, we have listened to students around us with a feminist ear becoming "attuned to those who are tuned out" (ibid). Students have approached us with their grievances, protests, and outcries, sharing stories of institutional abuse. Students, mostly from the Global South, have shared feelings of disappointment with poorly organized MA programs, which often charge burdensome tuition fees, and inappropriate and poorly researched feedback from the tutors. Some share their institutions' relentless attempts to exploit their traumas and stories to benefit the school's research agendas. One student recounted having an Israeli guest lecturer invited by their school to teach the history of Palestinian design; another student grieved about a presentation on political art of the Egyptian Revolution which featured propaganda images celebrating supporters of Egypt's deadliest military-led massacre.[1] Many complained about a program head recording students without their knowledge or consent for their own PhD research, and more.

These examples illustrate the violent reality of having to navigate Western institutions that happily accept international students and praise diversity on their websites while lacking any substantive resources and tools for the anti-racist, anti-discriminatory, and anti-oppressive education that is necessary. The students we encountered, desperate for allies, shared their sense of disillusionment and alienation with us, as their institutions continued to fail at listening to them, regarding them instead as objects of research and data for liberal agendas that bring money and prestige to their schools.

Failed attempts

Institutions that look beyond hiring a diverse team alone and aspire to decolonize the curriculum can still fail to provide and facilitate spaces and possibilities for decolonization. This is often the case when decolonization is seen as a bureaucratic checklist: a one-time lecture, an introductory note, a "diverse" book each term, or an isolated discussion that only concerns students interested in political work. Students are constantly asked to decolonize their practices without being given any tools or resources. Meaningful references beyond the canonical array of white men are absent. Decolonization remains an empty buzzword, since the institutions are apparently unable to genuinely engage in forms of transformative work and knowledge production—as inferred by the grievances sketched out above—which are crucial to decolonization (Bhambra 2018). In the case of design schools, this would mean an ontological recentering of education by situating it in relation to persistent structures of inequality, sexism, racism, and colonialism.

← cosmetic change/ empty gestures ← pg.65

[1] The massacre of Rabaa is a military-led massacre, which took place on August 14, 2013, in Egypt, in which unarmed supporters of the Muslim Brotherhood Party were attacked, leading to 817 documented casualties. See Patrick Kingsley, "Egypt's Rabaa Massacre: One Year On," *The Guardian*, August 16, 2014, https://www.theguardian.com/world/2014/aug/16/rabaa-massacre-egypt-human-rights-watch.

Mission Impossible

We still struggle in our work with well-intentioned colleagues who throw onto students the responsibility of bringing decolonization into the terminology they use, the design choices they make in their presentation slides, the references they present, the discussions they provoke, the topics they include or exclude, and the schools of thought and standards of design and practice they impose as good or bad. This can be particularly dangerous for first-year students, who come into art and design schools with inherited myths around hegemonic design standards being the measure of attainment. We are occasionally asked by design institutions to hold introductory sessions on decolonization and depatriarchalization. This often comes as a relief to the rest of the faculty, who feel satisfaction that the curriculum has finally been cleansed of its coloniality and patriarchy.

"I am really interested in talking with you. Could we continue having this conversation?"

"It's so great to listen to you, you have enlightened me."

"Thank you for bringing in your criticality, and questions of gender and decoloniality."

↖ pg. 119

We often hear these seemingly nice words of appreciation for our educational practices. However, even if superficially cordial, they once again put the burden of raising critical issues on us, and deflect the responsibility of undertaking the radical structural transformation of the institution. Our work is fraught. We lament that the compliments we receive for our interventions make us a decolonial/depatriarchal magical wand for the institution. The wand we have to repeatedly wave to call out the institution's unnamed aggressions: the blackface photograph appearing in a student's project; the uncritical use of "Chop Suey" fonts that convey a reductive caricature of "Asianness" for a ceramic tea-set designed in a first-semester industrial design course; or the overwhelming lack of references by and about women-of-color in course reading lists, to name a few offenses. It is an exhausting, frustrating, and extremely lonely task. And even at this task we often fail, by not reacting to yet again racist, sexist, or otherwise discriminatory comments or projects. These art and design institutions' attempts to decolonize the curriculum are disingenuous if there is no clear of what decolonization means. We are tired at, and unsurprised by, the fact that these institutions are not ready to be confronted with a definition that will pierce the fundamental understandings and assumptions upon which Western art and design are built. This would be a definition that renegotiates core standards of function and form, rethinks rubrics for evaluating taste and quality, and reflects critically on the values that motivate design in the first place. It has been too comfortable for too long to think that oppositional politics have no place in the classroom or in design practice, and that this problem may be baked into the design school irrevocably. The graduate show we attended in October reflected a reality of the design-school-as-factory, wherein isolated, dominant, value-free, apolit-

(myth of)
neutrality → ical design is reproduced mechanically in great volumes.

112

Hayfaa Chalabi, Maya Ober

accountability/
complicity →

While we acknowledge and address unjust power structures in the educational institution, we believe our positions as teachers inside the classroom remain complicit in reproducing sometimes violent, vertical learning experiences. We are faced with our own emotional exhaustion every time we need to explain white innocence, white saviorism, and/or unpack any student work that reproduces problematic narratives. While we claim to advocate for imagining alternative design futures, futures where more contextualized and just possibilities exist, our rage often inhibits us from imagining a non-violent classroom where we could create opportunities for generous feedback instead of a demonstration of discursive prowess.

While we believe that design education must be transformative, we are still struggling and learning what power structures we must avoid reproducing inside the classroom. If we wish to partake in dismantling powers that reproduce and praise problematic work, we must question and understand how we as teachers use our power. We tend to disregard multiple topics as ethical once proposed by students while wishing to equip ourselves with tools to help students reach those conclusions themselves. We still question our methods for creating an intentional space where students have the possibility of undertaking safe learning journeys no matter where they stand and what subjects they are interested in exploring.

While we problematize certain histories and subjects inside the classroom, we are still learning how to teach unjust histories without sharing materials that allow for the passive viewership of oppressed bodies. What gaze do we create spaces for inside the classroom while teaching about histories of the oppressed? What positions do we take in facilitating passive witnessing of structural injustice? While we believe that a liberating educational practice is a practice that does not see problematic student work as work created by people with bad intentions but rather as work created by people who are not equipped with tools that can liberate them from normative thinking, we must constantly equip ourselves with tools that question the way we use our power as teachers inside the classroom.

Works Cited

Al-Halabi, Diana. "Holding Palestine." May 2021. Accessed May 23, 2022. https://www.dianahalabi.com/holding-palestine.

Anania, Billie. 2021. "How Watermelon Became a Symbol of Palestinian Resistance." *Hyperallergic.* July 29, 2021. https://hyperallergic.com/666111/how-watermelon-became-a-symbol-of-palestinian-resistance/.

Ahmed, Sara. 2021. *Complaint!* Durham, NC: Duke University Press.

Barišić, Jelena. 2015. "Charlie In Zicht." *ver beton.* January 12, 2015. https://www.versbeton.nl/2015/01/charlie-in-zicht/.

Bhambra, Gurminder K., Dalia Gebrial, and Kerem Nişancıoğlu, eds. 2018. *Decolonizing the University.* London: Pluto Press.

Decolonising Design. 2016. "Editorial Statement" November 15, 2017. https://www.decolonisingdesign.com/editorial-statement.

DIWAN. 2021. *Institutional Solidarity.* Disarming Design. May 28, 2021. Archived on Internet Archive. Accessed May 26, 2022. https://archive.org/details/institutional-solidarity-set.

Katz, Phyllis A. 1996. "Raising feminists." *Psychology of Women Quarterly* 20, no.3: 323–340.

Keshavarz, Mahmoud. 2019. *Design Politics of the Passport: Immobility, Materiality, and Dissent.* London: Bloomsbury Visual Arts. 36, no.4: 20–32.

Khandwala, Anoushka. 2020. "What Does it Mean to Decolonize Design?" *Eye on Design,* June 5, 2019. https://eyeondesign.aiga.org/what-does-it-mean-to-decolonize-design

Lorusso, Silvio. 2021. "Notes on the WdKA's Removal of a Pro-Palestine Resistance Students' Banner." Institute of Network Cultures, *Entreprecariat,* May 18, 2021. https://networkcultures.org/entreprecariat/notes-on-the-wdkas-pro-palestine-resistance-banner-removal/.

Pink, Sarah. 2007. *Doing Visual Ethnography.* India, SAGE Publications.

Samarskaya, Ksenya. 2022. "Creative Director and Teacher Forest Young on Designing a More Inclusive Future." *Eye on Design,* May 17, 2022. https://eyeondesign.aiga.org/creative-director-and-teacher-forest-young-on-designing-a-more-inclusive-future/

Teaching

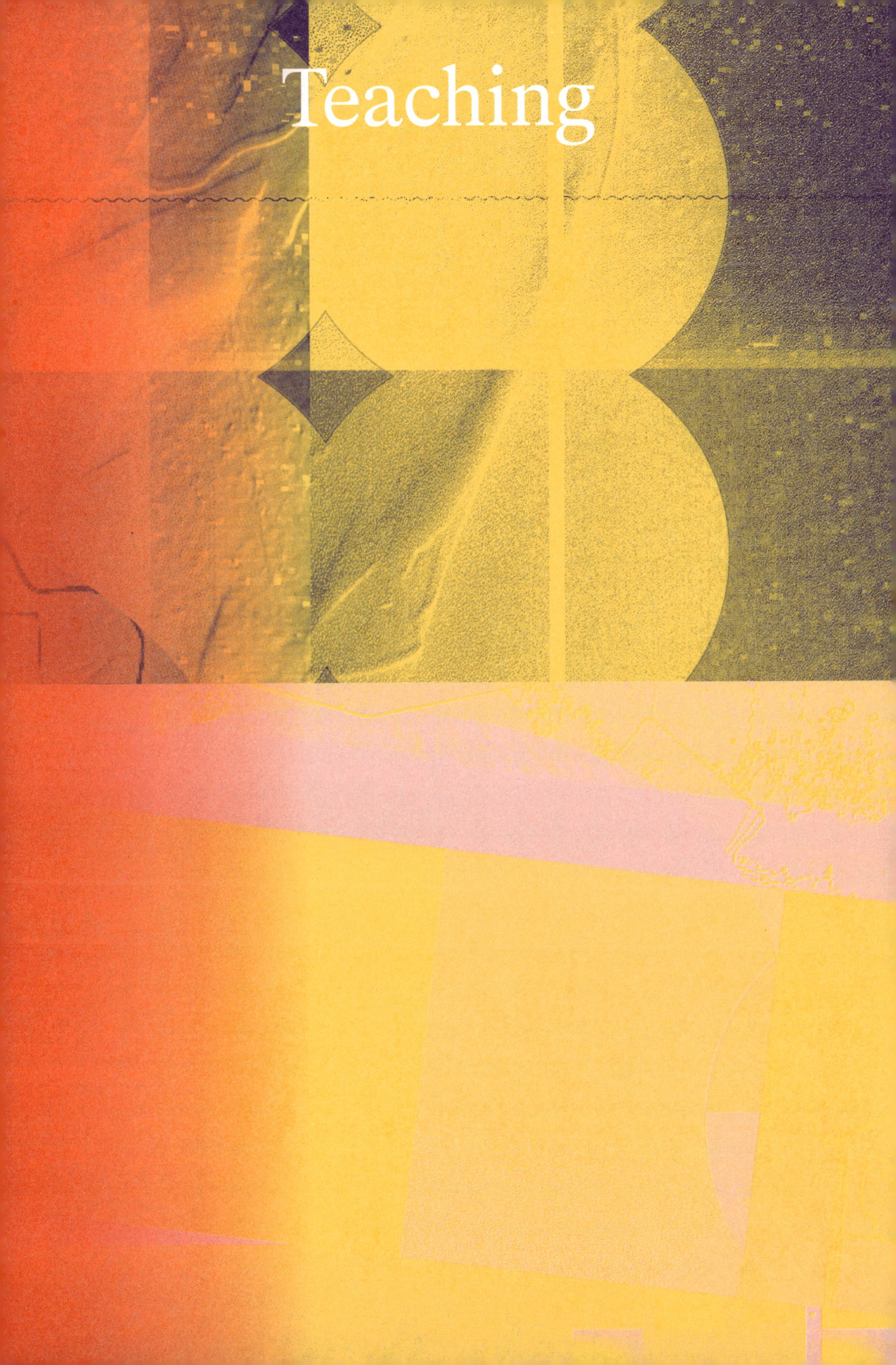

In the Service
of Decolonization

Uzma Z. Rizvi

Jul 2022

In so many ways, colonialism is the bureaucratization of inequality. If there was ever a way to create boundaries, hierarchies, and incomprehensible distinctions of merit, we may find that ideals of best practices, paperwork, and claims of process have played an integral role. Bureaucracy, in this regard, is the system that holds and maintains colonial power, and by extension, all those who participate in the system are also held in place. The relationship between new late liberal/ late capitalist models of racism and colonization is deep and complex (McLarren and Torres 1999). The racialized lives of people around the world today owe much of their conditions to a history of colonization that links economics as capital to human bodies, landscapes, and forms of understanding the self and others. Colonization was and continues to be an incredibly violent form of control that interlinks heteropatriarchy, capitalism, and the project of nationalism. Those same ideals found ways by which to be reiterated in the University; in fact, one might argue that it is precisely those ideals upon which a civilizing and disciplining mission of the University may be based (Sriprakash, Rudolph, and Gerrard 2022). The perversity of the colonial machinery is best observed in the use of bodies to maintain these systems of distinction; in that sense, service is required by all to maintain the workings of the disciplining machine.

There are, of course, so many of us who continue to study and work within these systems, which are clearly not designed for us. For those of us inhabiting bodies of difference, these systems create cognitive

← mechanisms of maintenance

← material condition of pg.40

117

dissonance; conditions that question our experiences and expertise. And yet, we persist, engaging, reworking, questioning, and striving toward reforming the bureaucracy and system. This desire to keep working, to undo that which holds inequality in place, is what defines one doing service in the service of decolonization. It is a deep desire to interrupt the harm, the violence, and the colonial apparatus. As la paperson has identified us, "these subversive beings wreck, scavenge, retool, and reassemble the colonizing university into decolonizing contraptions. They are scyborgs with a decolonizing desire" (paperson 2017, xiii).

reassembling →

structural agency of educator →

In so far as one might claim to be scyborg, that is, s+cyborg—la paperson's queer turn of the word "to name the structural agency of persons who have picked up colonial technologies and reassembled them for decolonizing purposes"—one is, in some measure, always in the process of an undoing and reassembling (xiv). What does it mean to undo in the context of the institute (here being used to gloss the university, holding within it the system and technologies of settler coloniality), within spaces of creativity, experimentation, and project-oriented pedagogies? What precisely are we looking to undo, and in the service of what? And perhaps more pragmatically, what comes after we are undone?

↖ pg.58

mainstream pedagogy; un-maintain/ undoing; reassembling →

Simultaneously, as la paperson reminds us, scyborg are created from colonial desire, exactly what the colonial machine purported to create from the uncivilized. But, as we are only made as a mimicry of an original university subject, our bodies always represent a deep anxiety, and hold the possibility of undoing everything in the name of decolonization. There is a very fine line many of us walk; one only has to think back to Franz Fanon's *Black Skin, White Masks* (1952) and how the deep colonization of the self comes to the fore to be confronted with the complexity of what being a scyborg might really mean. What are we trying to undo when we ourselves are defined by this system of oppression masked as a hub of knowledge?

inbetweener →

↖ pg.39

At this point in my career, I think quite deeply about the relationship between the service that I do, what the institute administration's job is, and who defines those positions. A core tension of this discussion is precisely this: if we can see the settler colonial logic within the Institute, why do we maintain it? The mechanisms of maintenance are what are colloquially glossed as "service." Service is directly related to labor outside the classroom that a faculty or teaching staff does to support the academic frameworks, policies, procedures, and systems established in the institution of higher education. My experience teaching as a full-time faculty for over a decade has led me to understand that there are different modes of service even under this umbrella term. In most university settings, the requirement to serve on committees in one's department or school is a contractual obligation, and certainly, depending on the institution, is considered a key component for tenure and review. This creates a condition wherein those who are teaching are expected to maintain the systems that allow for their pedagogical expressions.

← mechanisms of maintenance

labor →

If these systems are what support our pedagogies of resistance or decolonization, how can we expect an unjust system to uphold justice? If service is, indeed, faculty labor to keep the machine going, then how do we contend with the complicity of maintaining a system that we may not agree with, that is, a colonial system? Isn't that exactly what it means to be complicit in maintaining the violent structures of the academy?[1] If we continue to work for the academic-industrial complex, without undoing these forms, systems, and policies that uphold racist, classist, heteropatriarchal ways of doing, we are, in fact, complicit in the maintenance of the settler-colonial system. This essay takes its cue from this moment and presents an analysis of service that takes into account the ways by which service is proffered, and the ways by which we may reorient those bureaucracies in the service of decolonization.

accountability/
complicity →

↖ pg.107

It is also important at this point to be clear about the Global North/American standpoint of this text (and by extension mine, as author), written while living on unceded lands of the Lenape; this text is, as Marcelo Diversi and Claudio Moreira write, the work of a betweener, the "(un)conscious bodies experiencing life in and between two cultures" (Diversi and Moreira 2009, 19). In fact, it is often the betweener who finds themselves pulling together our realities on the scraps of colonial technologies, as we embody a code-switching scyborg to retool, reframe, rework, and transform our collective futures. While there is nothing normative about us, we come into the fray to work because we recognize the violence will continue on other bodies like our own.

← inbetweener

Understanding service as decolonizing, justice work for our students and the institute may explain why research shows that women and BIPOC scholars end up doing so much more service as care work for institutions (Guarino and Borden 2017). The colonial apparatus not only creates more work for us, it also insists that such work is of lesser value. It is lauded as necessary for all to do, but we find those with systemic power rarely do it because it does not serve their privilege—in the most explicit sense, it doesn't amount to much for promotion. This creates, within the scarcity model that the academy has been thrust into, a space within which the actual work that must be done is what is least valued. It is the work done by those who have lesser power that maintains their status as lower than those for whom such work is not required in equal measure.

labor →
↖ pg.57,
71,
108

There are affordances made to those with power: we hear it when excuses are made for their poor service performance, "For some people, service is not their strength," or "We all know their research is strong, even if they have a poor service record." This reflects a settler-colonial society: Who is responsible for the maintenance of the everyday at the institute? Who is cleaning our classrooms? Who is our security? In very much the same way, we find those bodies who do the work of maintenance of academic process are particularized (often BIPOC and women), and as such, this work is seen as having lesser value. And so, we are

normative
evaluation →

---

1   Here I am also thinking about the many conversations in *On the Re-Distribution of Power: Criticisms on Design Pedagogy* (The Teachers Project, Pratt Institute, 2020).

taught our academic value systems based on these hierarchies of colonial privilege.

mechanisms of maintenance; the priorities/ agenda of the school and nation →

I would like to argue that these values are also a part of the false logic and consciousness perpetuated by the settler-colonial academy in order to ensure that those most likely to launch institutional critique are the ones who want to stay far away from it and maintain themselves as disaffected. Protecting such critique is also the bureaucracy, the paperwork that defines the system that holds us all in place. For example, when proposing that we do something differently, I have often heard how exciting (in a theoretical sense) such work is, but that we do not have the system or structure to support such work. This happened routinely during my graduate education: I would propose a different way of teaching/learning, and the response would acknowledge that it was an exciting way forward that would/could decenter Western whiteness, but (and there is always the "but"), "we" cannot do anything to support it because there is no mechanism in place for it. And so I asked—how does one go about creating or changing that system? Long answers related to policy and service were brought forth. The subtext being that, as a researcher, you should focus on other things and leave this to upper administration.

But this is precisely the sort of service I believe in. I envision such reworking taking the form of transformative justice. Transformative justice is, at its core, the desire to respond to a form of violence without creating more violence. As a political framework, it comes from prison reform and abolitionist theory, but can be also used to think about what it might mean to engage in a transformative practice based in the desire to reduce and stop the replication of violence (Mingus, n.d.). Anyone who has taught in the academy knows that the replication of violence is embedded in the structures of teaching, for example, the ways by which we insist that our students replicate, cite, and know the classics, the core, the foundations.[2] Epistemologically, such iteration maintains a certain type of knowledge as central and all others as peripheral. As a scholar with vested interests in the historical frame, my argument does not rest on the elimination of foundations and the classics, but rather, on the creation of a space—if one

place →

can think of a syllabus as a space—that holds the multiplicity of significance within that moment. Simply, we must acknowledge that there

many other centers and peripheries →

are many other cores, classics, and peripheries. We must understand that the impact of history on the contemporary is important for us to contextualize in all of our disciplines; in order to teach it we must engage in epistemic critique. We must recognize that for our students, the lifting and celebration of a particular form of knowledge is often at the

↖ pg.66

expense, erasure, and replacement of their life experiences and histories. It is a particular sort of violence that pierces through their understandings of self, scarring them for life. I say this from experience, having found graduate school to be a remarkably traumatic experience, predominantly because my voice was continuously erased to replace it with the core, the foundations (Rizvi 2015).

---

2   Another example of such violence would be testing and grading. Learning should never be punitive. For a good overview of the case to be made against grading in higher education, see Jesse Stomell, "Ungrading: A Bibliography," author's website, March 3, 2020, https://www.jessestommel.com/ungrading-a-bibliography/. See also, Christopher Lee, "Against Grading," *On the Re-Distribution of Power: Criticism on Design Pedagogy* (New York: The Teachers Project, Pratt Institute, 2020), 27–41.

Uzma Z. Rizvi

In order to ensure that we are not replicating this violence, we must intentionally create strategies that interrupt the harm caused by the violence. In her book, *Emergent Strategies*, adrienne maree brown invites us to consider transformative justice as acknowledging the reality of the state of harm; looking for alternative ways to address/ interrupt harm, which do not rely on the nation-state; relying instead on organic, creative strategies that are community created and sustained; transforming the root cause of violence, not only the individual experience (brown 2017). It is important to recognize these are community-based activities—these forms of action require building solidarity across groups of people and learning how to trust and rely on one another.

collective action/
collectivity →

If there is any space for transformative justice, it is precisely here, in the space of service. For a reevaluation of such labor to take place, we have to understand precisely what this labor is doing, and why it is so dangerous for the system to value. When we work for decolonization—an undoing of colonial violence—in our classrooms, in our research, in the hallways, in faculty meetings, in all aspects of our work, we make the space more equitable for all. Service, then, is not work done only to maintain curricular functions, but rather, an ethic that informs all ways of being such that harm is not replicated. That is what must be valued. The only way to disrupt the bureaucracy of inequality is to reconsider what is valued. This is not done in the service of creating new hierarchies, but rather, with a consideration of how care, consent, and a lack of harm may, in fact, be a generative, rather than an extractive form of teaching and learning.

← unmaintain/
undoing

← care work
↖ pg.105

What then of our scyborg, who is both a manifestation of colonial desire and desires decolonization? Is there a way by which a generative pedagogy might ease the cognitive dissonance of existing in that space? I would argue that if we work in the service of decolonization, we no longer serve the settler-colonial institute and are not bound by its requirements of value. Do not be mistaken: it is not the neoliberal university that we are out to protect and save, it is the generations of bodies moving through these spaces that we are working to ensure a safe passage. In my mind, it is that valuable labor that we engage in when we speak of working in the service of decolonization.

unmaintain/
undoing →

Works Cited

brown, adrienne maree. 2017. *Emergent Strategy: Shaping Change, Changing Worlds*. Chico, CA: AK Press.
Diversi, Marcelo, and Claudio Moreira. 2009. *Betweener Talk: Decolonizing Knowledge Production, Pedagogy, and Praxis*. Walnut Creek, CA: Left Coast Press.
Guarino, Cassandra M., Victor M. H. Borden. 2017. "Faculty Service Loads and Gender: Are Women Taking Care of the Academic Family?" *Research in Higher Education* 58: 672–94.

McLaren, Peter, and Rodolfo Torres. 1999. "Racism and Multicultural Education: Rethinking 'Race' and 'Whiteness' in Late Capitalism." In *Critical Multiculturalism: Rethinking Multicultural and Antiracist Education*, ed. Stephen May, 42–76. London: Falmer Press.
Mingus, Mia. n.d. "Transformative Justice: A Brief Description." *Transform Harm*. Accessed December 13, 2021. https://transformharm. org/transformative-justice-a-brief-description/.

paperson, la. 2017. *A Third University Is Possible*. Minneapolis: University of Minnesota Press, 2017.
Rizvi, Uzma. 2015. "Being an Archaeologist." *The Story Collider*. July 17, 2015. https://www.storycollider.org/ stories/2015/12/31/uzma-rizvi-being-an-archaeologist.
Sriprakash, Arathi, Sophie Rudolph, and Jessica Gerrard. 2022. *Learning Whiteness: Education and the Settler Colonial State*. London: Pluto Press.

121

Design and Disillusion: A Starter Pack
Silvio Lorusso

In this talk, Silvio Lorusso shares his current research on the disillusionment permeating the design field. In his upcoming book, Lorusso interrogates self-deprecating memes, navigates generational resentment, and confronts the soul-crushing reality of everyday life within the creative industries.

Entreprecariat: Entrepreneurship and Precarity in Design

Two years ago, I wrote a book called *Entreprecariat*. The main thesis is basically contained in the title—in this portmanteau, this double word. Entrepreneurialism was and is turning a certain mode of operating in the world, the "entrepreneurial mode," into a system of value, a moral system, which interacts at various levels with precarity and mechanisms of precarization. This wasn't a book about design, but there are certain manifestations of entrepreneurialism and precarity in the design field. I'll use some examples to give you an idea of how the "entreprecariat" relates to design and what some of the consequences of such a relationship between these two terms might be.

mechanisms of maintenance →

The above was one of the descriptions of an event I was invited to, to speak about labor issues within design, before publishing the book. So you can already see a strong ideological language around developing your own profession. For example, you can see it in notions like "lifelong learning"—which on paper is really empowering-or the idea of disruption. These are things that we are very used to. In this case, it was very blatant—entrepreneurialism as a set of values—because they were using Joseph Schumpeter's expression of "entrepreneurial spirit" and layering it with a certain affective value.

Anthony Burril's "work hard & be nice to people" poster is one of the rare cases in which a designer's work becomes truly iconic and goes beyond the canon of the design field. In fact, it led to many rip-offs and bootlegs on Etsy.

This is a picture [of Burril's poster] by Francisco Laranjo taken in London's financial district, where it decorates the offices of business people, economists, and so on. What's interesting about this poster, and Burril's artwork, is that it brings together the traditional work ethic of working hard and sacrificing yourself for work, with the new spirit of the capitalist work ethic of putting enjoyment to work, putting a personal relationship into the work-and it's of course, the "be nice" part.

joy →

Another instance of this interrelationship between entrepreneurship and precarity in design is this book by Steven Heller and Lita Talarico, *The Design Entrepreneur: Turning Graphic Design into Goods That Sell*,[1] which was an overview of projects that were born out of the master's program they created. They wanted to emphasize this entrepreneurial direction of designers. In the description you see, it was a bit startling for me to find the two words, entrepreneur and precarious, in the same sentence within a design book.

1   Steven Heller and Lita Talarico, *The Design Entrepreneur: Turning Graphic Design into Goods That Sell* (Beverly, MA: Rockport Publishing, 2008).

When I define the constraints of my project

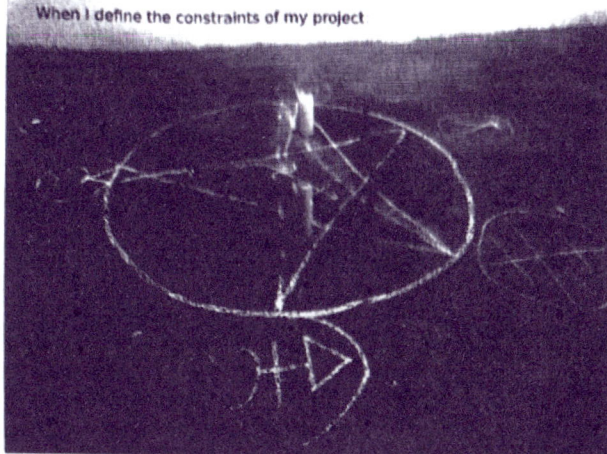

Finally, another book that somehow shows this ideology around entrepreneurship in the creative world is Gem Barton's *Don't Get a Job, Make a Job.*[2] You see it already from the title. Entrepreneurial ideologies have a lot to do with autonomy and independence, so you don't get a job, you *make* your own job. And there is generally a sort of doom-narrative starting premise, like the difficulty of finding a job. Landing a job is not the default anymore. This is a bit of a motivational book to deal with this situation entrepreneurially.

Starter Pack

Soon chaos will be our common denominator, we carry it within us, and we will find it simultaneously in a thousand places, everywhere chaos will be the future of order, order already no longer makes sense, it is nothing more than an empty mechanism and we wear ourselves out in perpetuating it so that it can consecrate us to the irreparable.[3]

        –Albert Caraco, *Brevario del caos* (Breviary of chaos)

According to Victor Papanek–early environmentalist, countercultural designer, and outspoken critic of US imperialism–design is "the conscious and intuitive effort to impose meaningful order."[4] Hence, tidying up a desk, curating a party playlist, structuring the chapters of a book–all of these activities can be understood as a design endeavor. It is distressing, however, to realize that very few human activities escape this definition. Are we all condemned to give a fragile order to things and imbue such order with a provisional, particular meaning, like an army of monomaniacal archivists in the Tower of Babel? And what about designers? How does the order they have been assigned to impose emerge?

If design is about order, its precondition is not void, but chaos.[5] Imposing a meaningful order begins with drawing the line that separates what is subject to the design effort from what is not: the former is what designers generally call the "problem." Design is a magic circle that produces an orderly inside and a chaotic outside, safeguarding and reworking the shifting border between the two, and finally placing things and people in one or the other. But the line is porous: our ordering attempt is inevitably artificial and its outcome necessar-

design problem solving; threshold →

2 Gem Barton, *Don't Get a Job... Make a Job: How to Make It as a Creative Graduate* (London: Laurence King Publishing, 2020).

3 Albert Caraco, *Breviario del caos* (Milan: Adelphi Edizioni, 1998). Translation mine.

4 Victor Papanek, *Design for the Real World: Human Ecology and Social Change* (London: Thames and Hudson, 1973), 4.

5 This is something that Mary Shelley was already pointing out in 1831: "Invention, it must be humbly admitted, does not consist in creating out of void, but out of chaos." The quote comes from a preface to her novel *Frankenstein, or The Modern Prometheus.* The plot seems to suggest that traces of chaos reside in the order, or even that order is chaos provisionally patched, like the body-corpse of the monster. Cited in Maria Popova, "'Frankenstein' Author Mary Shelley on Creativity," *The Marginalian,* June 25, 2028, https:// www.themarginalian. org/2018/06/25/mary-shelley-creativity-frankenstein-1831/.

ily unstable. Entropy corrodes the negentropic islands we call our projects. Order is always under siege. Chaos is lurking, regardless of whether we ignore it or not. Design's selective attention only partially works. If design as a method can be defined, the chaos that surrounds it can only be described through feelings and impressions.

6   A wicked problem is a problem that can't be unambiguously and definitively solved because its formulation is incomplete, shifting, or even contradictory. The term was coined by design theorists Horst W. J. Rittel and Melvin M. Webber in "Dilemmas in a General Theory of Planning," *Policy Sciences* 4, no. 2 (June 1973): 155–69.

7   It's not a coincidence that most design papers and essays begin by paying an introductory tribute to complexity.

Each problem is a wicked problem.[6] its resolution is temporary, its paradigm ever shifting, its focus evolving. How can one provide yet another abstract definition of the design process when the circumstances of a messy reality are so imposing? Design seems to be left with only one option: staring chaos in the eyes, going beyond the somewhat reassuring notion of "complexity."[7] For chaos is not complexity: complexity is a field in which various forms of expertise compete, and chaos is the repressed that returns when the experts fail. If, as James Bridle argues, "complexity is not a condition to be tamed, but a lesson to be learned,"[8] chaos is a lament that has nothing to teach.

8   James Bridle, *New Dark Age* (London, Verso, 2018), 138.

material condition of (design) chaos

Chaos has something to offer: uniqueness. Paraphrasing Tolstoy, whereas projects are all alike, every chaos is messy in its own way. So, what does the chaos at the periphery of design look like? To me, it appears more or less like this: a draconian series of InDesign paragraph styles, a lost Indexhibit site, a logo commissioned ironically on Fiverr, the new MoMA show curated by Paola Antonelli, a heart on an Instagram story by Bráulio Amado, a visit to the final thesis show at the Dutch Academy Eindhoven, a 404 error on a wrong jQuery URL on a static webpage, a bunch of riso-printed zines, the *Alliance Graphique Internationale*, an expiring non-EU visa, a weak eduroam wifi access point, a crowdfunded exhibition, a digital-only poster against the Anthropocene, visually rich 16:9 slide decks, a Linnmon-Lerberg IKEA desk traveling from one rented room to another, an unpaid internship report, a video essay with a North American female voice over, Arial Condensed, a Dinamo meme followed by a dank.lloyd.wright one, dusty Taschen mammoth volumes left at my dad's place, variable fonts, walking tote bags, people dressed like posters, handmade protest signs, Post-it, a reggaeton DJ set, Cinema 4D free assets, the reading time during a workshop, a Twitter hot take on the new CIA brand, a bachelor's thesis on transhumanism, a grainy jpeg of a Fronzoni catalog, an urgent email from an obnoxious client, an alignment error on a 1,200 print-run, incipient lumbar scoliosis, a MacBook Pro with Touch Bar, a copy of Karel Martens's *Printed Matter* next to Nick Srnicek and Alex Williams's *Inventing the Future*, a pair of Lidl flip-flops, an expired Adobe Creative Cloud subscription, the daily advice of Stefan Sagmeister, a coffee-stained funding application, the *e-flux* spinner pattern, a witty rip-off of the MAGA hat, ten-page portfolios (10mb max), a Unity-based exploratory "videogame," a Marcel Breuer tubular chair tried once in a corporate office, this very Markdown file edited in dark mode.

less
is more

more
or less

124

The "Basic Designer" Starter Pack.

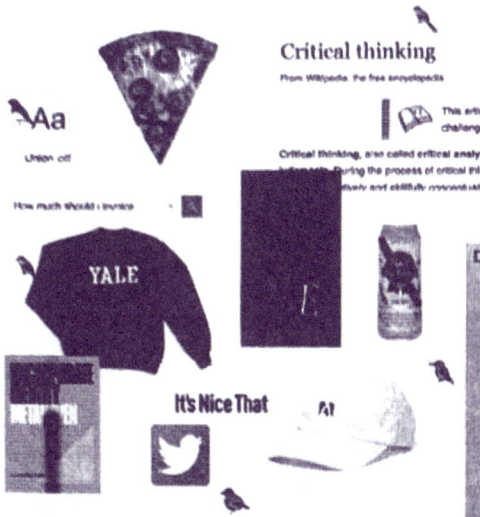

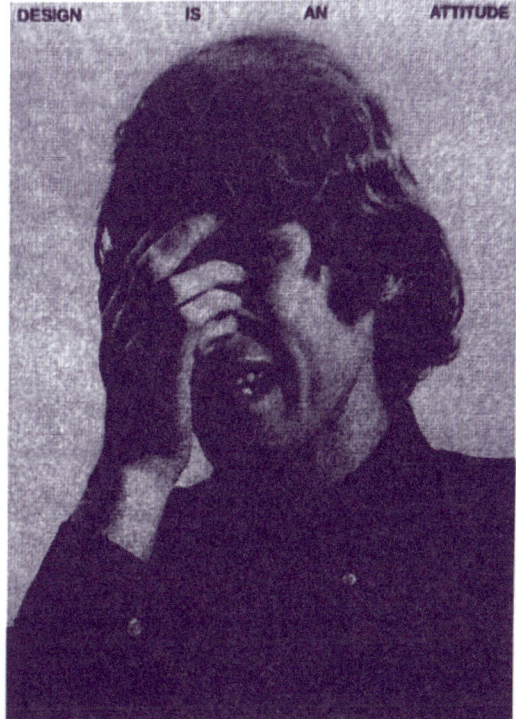

Someone familiar with design in the Global North (and probably elsewhere too) might share some of these elements in their personal design starter pack. "Starter pack" is the name of a meme in which the defining features of a certain profession, subculture, or fanbase are displayed against a white background.[9] They can be items, tools, books, or even habits. Often, clothes and accessories are included, showing that much of one's professional identity is inevitably based on conforming to a certain stereotype and signaling it. Online one can find many profoundly diverse starter packs for the designer category: "the graphic design student" pack, the "pretentious designer" one, the "pissing off a graphic designer" version... Actually, the radical statement of every starter pack is that there is no fundamental difference between tools, devices, literature, and clothes. Everything is an appendix of identity—something that contributes to a sense of belonging, and in some lucky cases, to the accumulation of prestige. The starter pack foregrounds what is unseen to the insider because it is mundane. For the outsider, unsurprisingly, the medium becomes the message. The starter pack meme highlights something else as well, namely, the fact that identity formation combines work and consumption. One is indeed tempted to go further and suggest that profession is, at least in part, a form of consumption. A chaotic assemblage of designerly stuff floating on a white canvas is supposed to alchemically generate personal character, personalized meaning. Mieke Gerritzen and Geert Lovink speak of "an aesthetic ambiance around your personality, filled with

aesthetic, identify →

material condition of representation and erasure →

9   "Starter Packs," Know Your Meme, accessed January 2, 2024, https://knowyourmeme.com/memes/starter-packs.

seductive ideas, things and experiences."[10] But this form of aesthetic identification is fragile. Another recent memetic formula reads: "designer is not a personality." There is a growing feeling that both work and consumption are insufficient means to build a solid, stable identity.

If we look specifically at graphic design, a dense, complex starter pack is the one built over three years on the Tumblr blog Critical Graphic Design.[11] There, one can scroll through a plethora of obscure inside jokes (some already outdated, as the blog shut down in 2015); an obsession with avant-garde designers who are also cultural producers, especially from the Netherlands, the UK, and the US (such as Experimental Jetset, Zak Kyes, and Michael Bierut); the parody of "criticality" as an attitude to display; some modified screenshots of the Photoshop interface; and non-existing "hyperstitional" theory books.[12] One can also notice the mechanism of self-canonization typical of small scenes, a fixation on Ivy League design schools such as Yale (but the logo of the Yale locks company is shown instead), the ironic indulgence in amateur design, a sensibility towards precarity and the hardships of the job market, and a few rants on the hypocrisy of political design, an acute awareness of consumerism and professionalism as two intersecting domains ("Everything is stuff"–whether a Metahaven book, a Nike Sneaker, or a Guy Fawkes mask). And finally, the traces of disillusionment ("roses are red violets are blue please please don't study graphic design").

High school friend: "My husband just got a promotion, I'm pregnant and we just bought our first house.

Me:

What the Critical Graphic Design group was suggesting, already five years ago, is that next to the visible lifestyle and professional items of design personality, there is a hidden starter pack,[13] one made of silent, sometimes unconscious entanglements: nightmarish bureaucratic procedures, financial troubles, rich families, gender biases, shitty clients, unpaid internships, dynamics of micro- or macro-celebrity, generous funding or lack thereof, a network of friends, gossip, and so on. These threaten or sustain the project of being able to develop projects–the professional life project of becoming a culturally active designer, and more crucially, of remaining one.

10 Mieke Gerritzen and Geert Lovink, *Made in China, Designed in California, Criticised in Europe: Design Manifesto* (Amsterdam: BIS Publishers, 2020). Originally, the subtitle of the book was *Amsterdam Design Manifesto*. This was an apt choice, as it situated the specific design chaos the authors describe. As I am also based in the Netherlands, I share strong elective affinities with their perspective. This is why their book will appear frequently in the coming pages. Whereas Gerritzen and Lovink focus mainly on the contemporary state of design, I concentrate on the state of *designers*, who are the first to be redesigned by it.

11 *Critical Graphic Design* (blog), accessed January 1, 2024, https://criticalgraphicdesign.tumblr.com.

12 "Hyperstition" is a term coined by writer and philosopher Nick Land. A portmanteau of the words "hyper" and "superstition," it suggests that ideas can be pushed into the cultural arena where they reinforce themselves, functioning as memetic self-fulfilling prophecies. See Delphi Carstens, "Hyperstition," Orphan Drift Archive, 2010, https://www.orphandriftarchive.com/articles/hyperstition/.

13 The hidden starter pack refers to the notion of hidden curricula theorized by, among others, John Dewey, Ivan Illich, and Paulo Freire. See Wikipedia, s.v. "Hidden Curriculum," last modified October 7, 2023, https://en.wikipedia.org/wiki/Hidden_curriculum.

...

Chaos precedes design and operates inside of it; it is the manifestation of the Real beyond the designerly illusion of a stable and durable order.

The Fragility of Design Projects and the Growing Sense of Disillusionment in Design

The "starter pack" can be enlarged or shrunk depending on the angle from which we look at the design project. The very idea of the constraint that defines the project is a consensual fiction, a consensual decision.

...

In general, what I'm trying to point out is the fragile threshold of what we call a "project"–the "definition of a design problem"–and the fact that there is a growing realization that this threshold is consensual and ritualistic to a certain extent, that there is something esoteric about it. I guess this gives you a bit of an idea of the diagnosis.

← threshold of "problem"

In the fragility of this consensus is the creation of an inside and an outside. There is a growing sense of disillusionment. I want to show you how I sense this and probe it in the rest of the world I am looking at.

First of all, in popular culture. You can say that there is a kind of bonding mechanism to show disillusionment with respect to design and, specifically, graphic design. Design-hating is, to a certain extent and in certain circles, becoming a way to create a sort of belonging. This is not necessarily negative per se, as it may be a way to open up to different views of design. Other things I find very relevant include the fact that the medium for doing this is memes, tweets, and other things that don't really belong to the visual culture of design. They don't generally look like posters that state how disillusioned their creators are about design. So, there is even a rejection of the culture of design in the making of those things.

← disillusion of design

But this is a horizontal level of popular culture–not that high culture, like the high echelons of design, are doing any better.

For example, in an email sent out to the PhD in design list, in which Don Norman picked up on Papanek's claim that industrial design is one of the most harmful industries. It's true, but only to a certain extent, because designers don't actually have that much power in the hierarchy of organization.

← structural agency of designer

John Maeda who I, of course, highly admire–it's hard not to admire the work of John Maeda–has been creating design impact reports every year, which are really, really insightful. But it's also interesting to see, year by year, how they change and what aspects vary. Of course, in 2017, "learn to code" was one of the highlights of the design field. Then for John Maeda, at least, writing became this sort of unicorn skill. And in 2019, finally, he had this sort of epiphany and started to say that after years of advocating for design labs in companies, he was starting to realize that maybe it's not such a great idea. That design is not so central and crucial within companies, within design organizations.

I am sharing other examples also to show that this is not necessarily a US-specific sentiment. Giovanni Lussu is an Italian designer and theorist, and his disillusionment has been towards the idea that much of the work of graphic designers, to a certain extent, only benefits themselves and their own culture. And he was saying this in 2012. Another example comes from Enzo Mari, a utopian. He was an artist before, and he became a designer because he believed that art didn't produce the transformational change needed to change the world. But then, after a decade or two of work, he started to doubt that the designer was the center of this transformational change. So he published an advert in a big Italian design magazine in which he was desperately seeking an entrepreneur, highlighting the fact that the central figure of transformational change within companies and firms is the entrepreneur. So he was sort of disillusioned in this sense, with centrality and hierarchy.

revolutionary →

Finally—and this is the most troublesome perspective on this disillusionment—it is statistical. I was looking at the AIGA Design Census for 2019. What can be derived from it is that one out of three designers is, partially at least, dissatisfied with their job. What we don't see in this statistic is also the dropouts. People really said, "I can't take this anymore," so I suspect that if we considered this phenomenon more broadly, the rate of dissatisfaction would be higher.

structural agency of designer →

From Delusion to Dilution to Disillusionment

Disillusionment is the starting point, and I think this disillusionment has to do with two steps that preceded it. One is dilution, this solution of the design profession. Even before that, there are a series of illusions that are being slowly shattered, and we start to sense more and more that they were delusions.

Technical and Methodological Dilution of Design

popularization of design thinking →

I think design is diluted in two ways. One is technical and the methodological. If I had to use two allegories, I would relate them to the magic wand and the Post-it note. The magic wand points at a technical delusion. Of course, this is almost common sense. By this, I mean that a lot of the design work flow, especially in visual design, is incorporated in the tools. The desktop publishing revolution was the moment in which this happened, or at least when this became more concrete.

Stack of	Design Delusions
power	that designers have power and authority within organizations
control	that designers have control on the conception and reception of their products
influence	that designers can affect the cultural industry and generate awareness (cfr. design for debate)
nature	that design is an ahistorical quality constitutive of human nature (cfr. Margolin)
autonomy	that design is mainly an economically sustainable profession rather than a lifestyle, a personality, an attitude
existence	that the thing we call design is an unambiguously identifiable "thing"
recognition	that the value of designers is socially recognized
stability	that the results of designers' effort are durable
order	that the space of the project is an orderly, controllable terrain
centrality	that design is the one discipline bridging all the others

128

On the Post-it side, we have a methodological dilution, and it appears in even the most successful contemporary design of the last year, which is of course "Design Thinking." Design Thinking has been extremely successful at bringing design outside of the design sphere, but at the same time, it has led to a situation in which Design Thinking—the methodology for thinking of problems as design problems—becomes assimilated to other disciplinary fields. The case in point is the fact that business students now study Design Thinking as part of their program. Design Thinking is not necessarily produced by designers themselves, so it's diluted in the sense that it is so successful that it relegates the designer to the side. That's the brilliance of it.

Another methodological delusion has to do with the idea of self-design—basically, turning design into a kind of self-help methodology to redesign your life. There are plenty of books that insist on this idea. Beatriz Colomina and Mark Wigley already clearly realized this in 2016, a wonderful book called *Are We Human?*[14] In it they say that design has gone viral, but it's a dangerous kind of success; it's a success in which design becomes, in a way, more successful than designers.

14 Beatriz Colomina and Mark Wigley, *Are We Human? Notes on Archeology of Design* (Zurich: Lars Müller Publishers, 2016).

structural agency of designer

Design Delusions
And now to the delusion part, which is also the most difficult one to approach, because there are so many things to say.

The Virgin "can you make the logo biggy?"   The Chad "with great power comes great responsibility!"

Design Double Bind

Delusion about Power
We saw it with Don Norman and John Maeda, who expressed this initial skepticism about authority within the organization.

Delusion about Control
By control, I mean the reception and conception of artifacts. In a way I think it's legitimate to say that a big part of the design profession has moved from clear necessities, from a logic of transforming the world by means of mass production in the traditional Bauhaus mode of operation, to wanting to influence, change behavior, and change the world by means of cultural production. So from mass production to cultural production, the shift maintains the same mechanism of broadcasting culture, as if culture was an item to be sold to a certain public. We still think of cultural production, to a certain extent, as a form of mass production, while of course the interpretation, the way in which culture is produced, is way more interactive and consumerist.

profitability of design →

Delusion about Influence

speculation/
imagination →

Many of the currents born in the last decade-design fiction, speculative design, design for debate-insist on one point. They say: What we do affects the world by raising awareness or creating debate. To a certain extent, I guess this is true, but I think Francisco Laranjo makes a crucial point. He says that it's not so much creating debate as it is about reducing debate

↖ pg.58

to a very narrow idea of what debate is, specifically, press releases, short semi-critical interviews, and so on. So instead of fostering debate, we have a narrowing down of what debate means. To be honest, I've been reading quite a few books that describe those projects, and I've always been disappointed by the fact that they engage with them at face value. They never go into this actual debate. They never show how much this debate has actually happened.

...

Much of this big delusion is more of a misunderstanding, which has to do with the conceptualization of design as a generic human activity. Recently, I've been reading this book called by Mike Monteiro, *Ruined by Design*, which is a very sincere and heartfelt book about ethics in design, especially in the context of tech. But what he says is this: if you are affecting how our product works in any way whatsoever, you are a designer, you are designing. So the budget holder becomes the designer, anybody who has a certain influence on it becomes the designer. The larger scope of this argument was made by the art historian Victor Margolin. And of course, you cannot deny that what he says is true-the fact that we as humans are designing species. But there is a big gap between this idea that "humans design"

threshold of
design →

and the specific culture of industrial design that, nowadays, we just call "design." This is something that Papanek was bringing to the table, that in the beginning, there was *design* but not *industrial design*. There is a mismatch in understanding. It's like, we think that this generic human activity has the same logic, the same principle, the same philosophy as something that was born a century ago. I think it's part of the mismatch because this philosophy of design, in the strict sense, is not recognized by the world at large.

I think it's very important to say that design is understood mainly as a profession, as a work, as a job. And I would like to insist on the fact that I believe that in the current context-and this is not to diminish the work of designers, which I appreciate and like-designing society fundamentally, on a large scale, is another thing-more like a hobby, a lifestyle, a feature, more of a personality trait, an interest. In a very obvious sense, everybody is interested in design, to a certain extent. We all know that you don't need to be a professional designer to appreciate the Apple design. It would be good to see professional designers and a minoritarian perspective on design. And of course, there is the more concrete issue of making a living, calling it a profession. An example of this is Justin McGuirk's exposé of interior design and product design, that reveals that there is a big facade in the profession.

130

Teaching

Design Double Bind: On the
Responsibilization of Design

inbetweener → I want to conclude by pointing out a mechanism that I believe is very strong in creating a sense of this delusion, which I call the Design Double Bind. The term double bind comes from anthropologist Gregory Bateson, and it refers to the idea that you get a signal from society or from a person, and at the same time, at the same level, you get a conflicting one. For example, I tell you I love you all the time, but then when it comes to physical affection, I'm very rough and maybe even show disaffection. This generally causes trauma. And I think this happens a lot in design, so there is a whole infrastructure of meaning that highlights power and responsibilization. The general slogan is this: "With great power comes responsibility." (You know the uncle of Spiderman, who is often quoted in design presentations?) At the same time, there is a reality check made of lack of recognition, and so on and so forth. I think it's through this very mechanism that a sense of disillusionment and trauma, professional trauma, comes to the fore.

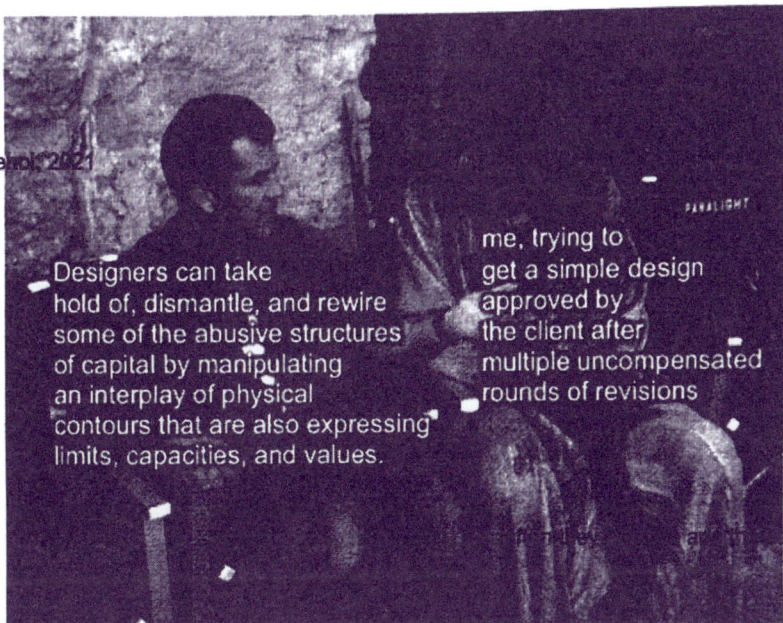

@neuroticarsehol 2021

Designers can take hold of, dismantle, and rewire some of the abusive structures of capital by manipulating an interplay of physical contours that are also expressing limits, capacities, and values.

me, trying to get a simple design approved by the client after multiple uncompensated rounds of revisions

The maestro of this kind of critique is neuroticarsehol," Twitter-Instagram person I don't know personally. They are very powerful in showing this double bind. I wanted to show this [image above] because they do it best. On the left, you see the theoretical self-aggrandizing and self-empowering view of responsibilization of design; inbetweener → designers [designers can take hold of, dismantle, and rewire some of the abusive structures of capital by manipulating an interplay of physical contours that are also expressing limits, capacities, and values), and then on the right, the most con-crete daily reality. One aspect I think is crucial is that very often, these two narratives reside in the same person, in the same reality. I see it myself when I have to do a WordPress theme development and then a presentation in which I like to push for this very empowerment of design. I think that that's the logic, mainly.

And finally, another micro-mechanism inside of the mechanism is an abuse of the word responsibility or responsibilization.

> Design is a craft with responsibility. Design is also a craft with a lot of blood on its hands every cigarette ad is on us. Every gun is on us. Every ballot a voter can understand is on us.[15]
>
> —Monteiro

15 Mike Monteiro, *Ruined by Design: How Designers Destroyed the World, and What We Can Do to Fix It* (San Francisco: Mule Design, 2019).

This feels a bit out of place, a bit out of proportion. I think that this is a form of field aggrandizement by over-responsibilization. In his book, Monteiro's demonstration is unable to provide any example of a good-doing or evil-doing that is enacted by someone who defines themselves within the design [field]. For example, the main evildoer is an engineer for Volkswagen. Those are the examples he brings in. There isn't even a negative way to demonstrate that power, so this power is probably lacking.

Interview with Silvio Lorusso

In your talk you tried to distinguish design
from the designer, asking us to think beyond
an insular perspective and reflect on our
roles in the practice. For instance, "design
thinking" commodified the process of design
practice and made "design more successful
than designers," while alternative routes
such as speculative design simply reduced
problems to the "debate." Are we doomed
to continue to offer an idealized vision
of design to secure a place in the flow
of capital? Where are design and designers
heading?

Sept 2023

Silvio In different ways and in different contexts, design is
becoming "stand-alone," independent from the designer.
A couple of examples: Design thinking morphed into a sort of liberal art taught to business school aspiring managers. Graphic design, both as a set of techniques and as a culture, is increasingly packaged within frameworks, platform editors, and AI systems. This is how "expert design" becomes "diffuse," to use Ezio Manzini's terminology.

Given this premise, "offering an idealized vision of design to secure a place in the flow of capital" is far from something designers are "doomed" to do—they're actually in luck if they manage! What do we mean, concretely, by "offering an idealized vision of design?" We mean convincing the public of the value of designers' expertise and authority. This form of lobbying takes the form of professionalization. We can say that design professionalization followed two routes.

↖ professionalization
of design

133

Let's borrow from Max Weber to identify these routes. First, design grounded its professional authority in rationality—think of the designer as a "scientific" problem solver (in the 1950s advertisers attempted the same). Second, design tried to legitimize itself through charisma—think of the allure of the designer as author, the lifestyle recommendations of Stefan Sagmeister, the cult of Philippe Starck, etc. So far so good. However, this is where things get interesting. Designers have managed to pull off a magnificent feat: they consciously transfigured the rational authority into the authority of charisma—*charismatic rationality*, if you will. Design demigods such as Massimo Vignelli, Paul Rand, and Dieter Rams have erected an aesthetic of simplicity and rationality rooted in visionary leadership. I wonder what a Weberian interpretation of modernism would yield...

As professional recognition along these lines vacillates, I believe yet another conversion of authority is taking place. Designers are attempting to gain cultural authority. This differs slightly from the blend of the rational and the charismatic I just described. Cultural authority turns the technical into the humanistic. Let me give you an example: if you're a graphic designer and you're able to be paid properly while using Comic Sans, you're successfully asserting your cultural authority. Unfortunately, however, this is unattainable at scale. This is why I believe that, at this point, designers, design theorists, design writers, and educators should seriously tackle the question of technics. Comic Sans is less an "inappropriate," "vernacular" font than an instance of the diffused technicity of graphic design. It shows how the threshold of what we refer to as the "technical" shifts. Writing an email in the '90s meant you were a tech-savvy person, an *expert*; today it means you're just an average computer user. The technicity of such practice has faded into the background. What technicities have dissolved in design? Which ones need to be foregrounded again?

I think it's also time to surpass the proto-shamanic idea of

← threshold

134

the designer as someone who spontaneously synthesizes different perspectives. This is another idealized vision that doesn't hold at scale. Not many designers are in that position. Focusing on the technical means interrogating the practical domain of design, the tacit dimension of the designer's activity. It means asking what role designers play, concretely, in shaping technologies, whether apps or institutions, but also what their actual place in the social structure of organizations is.

structural agency →

↖ pg.118

> You've spoken on the inflation of design's
> impact and the disproportionate responsibi-
> lity assigned to designers. In other words,
> considering design's proximity to power, are
> designers just tools for other forces? Or
> is there still some possibility to intervene?
> Drawing on your discussion on the over
> responsibilization of design, how does a
> "responsible" design curriculum reflect the
> priorities of the school and the nation?
> How would you sum up the agenda(s) of design
> schools in the Global North?

schooling/ university; responsibilization of design →

Silvio First of all, I would look for ways to measure such presumed proximity to power. How much agency does a product designer, say, at Amazon actually possess? Does this agency manifest within their design activity, that is, within the products they design, or outside of it, for instance through demands related to working conditions? The problem I see with the "responsible" or "ethical" approach to design is that it is rarely focused on design itself. Consider Mike Monteiro's recent book on design ethics: he barely mentions any cases of unethical design by designers. Instead, he discusses Volkswagen's manipulated emission tests. The evil character in this story is not the designer, but the engineer. We shouldn't ignore this.

structural agency →

↖ pg.52

Before ethics and responsibility in a practice comes the practice itself. We're all relieved when a design studio pays their interns decently, but this doesn't tell us much about the so-called role of design. Most activist design faces the same problem: it is stuck in the humanistic, declarative register of outrage. Its job is to assert what's wrong and give form to such assertions. When internet users do more or less the same thing that activist designers do, for instance, by posting a black square on their Instagram profiles, we become aware of the dilution of design into communication at large.

At one point in his 1970s book on design hope, Tomás Maldonado speaks of "the designer *as designer*." How does a designer behave ethically or responsibly *as a designer*, and not as a generic citizen or netizen? This is a fundamentally philosophical question—a dilemma, really, already formulated decades ago. Vilém Flusser's perspective on the matter is not so reassuring. In a lecture, he states that "responsibility is so widely diluted that in effect we are in a situation of total irresponsibility for the acts committed by industrial production." Perhaps it is more interesting to begin with this irresponsibility. How does it disseminate? At what point does the gap between intentions and possible actions become too wide? These considerations are valuable because they might lead to an "object-oriented" idea of ethics. Here, artifacts such as products, services, and organizations have politics that manifest in an operational manner, that is, in the way they work. This is why they're hardly even perceivable as politics. In this context, the designer's intentions are not what matters most, especially when those intentions are declared rather than implemented through decision making. Here's an ethical question: how do words become things? ← material condition of

> Can you share more thoughts on your
> understanding of craft as "a good job well
> done" and on the valorization of craft?
> ＼ craft

Silvio The definition of craft as "a good job well done" comes from sociologist Richard Sennett. I like it because it's agnostic, so to speak, in relation to the activity at hand: you can

136

apply such a definition to the work of carpenters as well as to that of Linux programmers, which is indeed what Sennett does. A craft offers the practitioner the possibility of being reflected in the object of their work. The thing they do becomes an anchor of identity in a society in which, for better or for worse, people identify with their work and job.

The opposite of a craft is a mindless, alienating activity that denies the very possibility of doing something well because it's someone else's "well." Hence, it is also not a "good job." Design is traditionally linked to a division of labor that separates the planner from the maker, the one who manages from the one who executes. In this sense, design is the professionalization of planning. In theory, once this happens there is no craft anymore because both the planner and the executor are alienated from their work—the former stuck in the merely abstract, the latter in the merely concrete.

professiona
lization of
design →

But things aren't so symmetrical. An executor has little escape from alienation. The planner, on the other hand, has several chances to work as a craftsperson. Enzo Mari once curated an exhibition on prototypes to demonstrate that the prototype room in a company is a bit like a medieval workshop, where practitioners think, plan, and make before the division of labor breaks it all apart for production at scale. The figure of the creative coder is another contemporary manifestation of the craftsperson: they are not only busy with the surface of interfaces but also active in conceiving and building entire applications, perhaps at the level of prototype, leaving the full implementation of the product to the company team. Here, we reach an almost paradoxical conclusion: the more designers are professionalized, that is, legitimized as professionals, the more they can be craftspeople.

Finally, the notion of craft resonates with me personally. These days, I'm reading about the life of C. Wright Mills, who was a bit of a designer himself. Actually, more than a bit: he wrote books in the morning and fixed his motorbike, baked bread, or repaired his house in the afternoon. Unfortunately, I'm not that versatile, but I appreciate Mills's understanding of writing as "intellectual craftsmanship," that is, as "the joyful experience of mastering the resistance of the materials with which one works." In most cases, the academic world removes that joy while in- ← joy creasing resistance, for both rational reasons (e.g., standardizing the structure of papers) and bureaucratic ones (e.g., measuring impact). To me, intellectual craftsmanship means keeping form and content together, paying attention to the register, the style of my writing as a way of experiencing it as my own. Once again, this connects to the issue of professionalization. I once read a study that shows that researchers in lower ranks use more jargon and more convoluted structures in order to signal their belonging to their scientific community, while more established scholars feel freer to write in an accessible way. Luckily, given design's pride in interdisciplinarity and practice, one's writing can be taken seriously without having to rely too much on esoteric language.

> In your talk, you say that building toward
> a craft provides a sense of stable identity,
> and is a way to combat the "dilution" of
> design. If identity is created by craft
> or connected through ways of making, when
> will one facet of our identity overpower
> the others? If craft can create a sense
> of belonging and stability, could individual
> perspectives be marginalized by dominating
> voices, resulting in hegemony (like with
> typography "nerds")?

Silvio Identity is a patchwork, but Western societies put a particular emphasis on its job component, the "What do you do?" question. Nerdiness can be seen as a reaction to that: I don't identify with what I do for a living, so I'll identify with, say, magic cards, displaying passion through erudition. Typography and type design, in particular, are interesting examples of identity being

138

enriched rather than flattened by crafty nerdiness. The community is very lively, but it is not just fonts fonts fonts—it deals with sophisticated questions of representation, from the presence of women designers to the development of Arabic typefaces.

craft; capitalism → This route of using craft centers making thingsand tools. Under capitalist logic, well-crafted things get framed and packaged as design, thus becoming sellable. Connecting this to your previous work on the entrepre-cariat, how do you think about the mindset of constant production? How do the tools constrain or liberate making? Can you speak to the possibilities and pitfalls of the valorization of craft and as a priority in design pedagogy?

Silvio To answer your question, it might be interesting to look at making very broadly. Let's consider internet platforms. I believe that one of their abilities is to turn making into speaking. They provoked or manifested a sort of linguistic turn. Using Hannah Arendt's term, the *homo faber* (*man the maker*) has been reduced to a shadow of the *zoon politikon* (*the political animal*).

threshold → The web became mainstream through users who acted like craftspeople: they designed and fabricated their personal webpages in relative isolation (a fundamental necessity for the homo faber, according to Arendt). With the advent of the blogosphere, Web 2.0, and later, social media like Facebook, poietic activity—making—became peripheral: from now on, only designers and programmers would craft webpages. The relative isolation that characterized, for instance, the "webpages of one's own" on GeoCities became a thing of the past as well. Facebook is in fact often compared to an *agora* in which people express themselves and discuss. If Web 1.0 was the laboratory of the one who makes, Web 2.0 is the *piazza* of the one who speaks. For Arendt,

collective action → speaking is what leads to action. It is *praxis*. However, on social media platforms, we mostly get speech without action. Tweeting is like giving an oration in the dark: one doesn't know exactly who is out there, and it may be that nobody is listening.

What other online activities can users dedicate themselves to? Now that the web has become a professional environment, any attempt to design and decorate an autonomous space on the internet feels amateurish. In this sense, I believe that nostalgia for the vernacular internet and the apology for online "brutal- ← aesthetic ism" are not coincidental. Most users are left with political expression (again, in a broad sense) that doesn't, however, coincide with initiative—they are left to contend with an arena of opinion sharing and with the reification of thoughts and passions. Much design work is political in this very narrow sense—it is declarative, expressive. The activist poster is akin to the political post. Rooting design in craft means going beyond the bold statement, the declaration, the manifesto. The driving question is a simple one: how can you use it?

The pitfall of craft is nostalgia, and design culture is ridden with it. Woodblock printing, risography, handmade bookbinding...the risk is to suggest that cute, old, or obsolete techniques ← pg.79 can shelter us from our overwhelming present. That's the design equivalent of what Geert Lovink calls "European offline romanticism." Craft shouldn't be deceptively pre-digital, but consciously post-digital, that is, critical of digital technology and its guiding ideologies. It should be embedded in the present time and re-shuffle notions of the cutting edge and passé: a lot of hi-tech software doesn't allow you to develop a craft, only to become a pro-user dependent on the tool.

If, as you say, "chaos precedes design and ← pedagogy of chaos operates inside of it," what might a pedagogy of chaos and a pedagogy of order look like? What's teachable?

Silvio "A pedagogy of chaos" ... I like the sound of that! My insistence on chaos has to do with the fact that design's promise

140

profession-
ization of
design →
of orderliness is seldom, if ever, fulfilled. Nowadays, the trendy term that you find in most paper, abstracts, and design events descriptions—"complexity"—doesn't go very far. Because, after all, complexity is reassuring: it suggests that there are experts who can make complexity readable, understandable, and thus simple. That mess can be tamed.

A pedagogy of chaos understands design as witchcraft: design is an elastic magic circle wherein constant negotiation takes place. What is order? What's entropy? Who decides what's what? Are you, as a designer and an individual, inside or outside the circle? A pedagogy of chaos doesn't only enlarge the magic circle; this would lead to a paranoia of total interconnectedness where every artifact needs to be grasped in its interaction with all others, where every problem needs to be linked to a larger problem, where every system needs to be understood through its relations with every other system. A pedagogy of chaos is, therefore, also able to tactically shrink the magic circle, because it understands that conceptual inclusion comes at a cost: it takes time and energy.

Finally, a pedagogy of chaos questions the covert, conservative attitude implied by the very notion of order. Not only does order appear provisional and brittle, it also limits design's pro-
time →jective potential. Order is the past casting its shadow; it is an instrument of what philosopher Tony Fry calls "defuturing."

Bios

post-radical pedagogy

Nida Abdullah, Chris Lee, and Xinyi Li are Associate Professors in the Undergraduate Communications Design Department at the Pratt Institute.

post-radical pedagogy (post-rad) is a research collective formed in 2020 dedicated to questioning the hostile aspects of educational administration and the colonial values embedded in design pedagogy. post-rad critically examines the design of curricular structures and explores alternatives to traditional syllabi, grading rubrics, classroom conventions, and the dynamics of authority. Their praxis spans teaching, research, creative scholarship, and academic service, particularly in the areas of curricular development and assessment. The term "post" encourages a reflection on inherited pedagogical conditions, acknowledging the ongoing struggle to articulate what a genuinely radical pedagogy in design might entail.

Cultivating reflective dialogue through various means—gathering as a form of critique, installation as onsite publishing, and slow publication as facilitation—post-rad aims to bring into discourse the otherwise illegible critical inquiry and knowledge production that take place within the banal and reductive frameworks of bureaucratic educational institutions.

Ahmed Ansari

Ahmed Ansari is an industry assistant professor in the Integrated Design & Media program at NYU Tandon. He holds a PhD in design studies from Carnegie Mellon University, a master's in interaction design, and a bachelor's in communication design from the Indus Valley School of Art and Architecture. His research interests intersect between design studies and history, philosophy of technology, critical cultural studies, and postcolonial and decolonial theory, with an area focus on the Indian subcontinent.

Danielle Aubert

Danielle Aubert is the author of *The Detroit Printing Co-op: The Politics of the Joy of Printing* (Inventory Press, 2019), *Marking the Dispossessed* (Passenger Books, 2015), and *16 Months Worth of Drawings in Microsoft Excel* (Various Projects, 2006). She is co-author, with Lana Cavar and Natasha Chandani, of *Thanks for the View, Mr. Mies* (Metropolis Books, 2012). She is a professor of graphic design at Wayne State University in Detroit. Since 2021 she has served as president of AAUP-AFT Local 6075, a union representing over 1,700 faculty and academic staff at WSU. From 2013 to 2015 she was a Fellow in the Creative and Performing Arts program at the Lewis Center for the Arts at Princeton University. She is a 2021 Kresge Award recipient.

Hayfaa Chalabi

Hayfaa Chalabi is an illustrator and educator interested in the role of illustration to recontextualize narratives, histories, and discussions. Chalabi uses her power as an illustrator and storyteller to spark discussions about different sociopolitical issues. Her work revolves around the intersections of visual culture, sexuality, gender, and migration. Prior to her latest research project, "Refugees Welcome?: A Study of Structural Apathy towards Refugees in Sweden," Chalabi conducted the study "Your Exotic, Your Victim, Your Terrorist: Visual Storytelling to Challenge the Western Stigma of Arab Women in Areas of Conflict," which focused on the case of Raqqa in Syria during its total occupation by the Islamic State in 2014. Currently, Chalabi works as a senior lecturer at the University of the Arts London.

John Jennings

John Jennings is a professor, author, graphic novelist, curator, Harvard University Fellow, *New York Times* bestselling author, 2018 Eisner Winner, and all-around champion of Black culture. As professor of media and cultural studies at the University of California at Riverside, Jennings examines the visual culture of race in various media forms including film, illustrated fiction, comics, and graphic novels. He is also the director of the Abrams ComicArts imprint Megascope, which publishes graphic novels focused on the experiences of people of color. His research interests include the visual culture of hip-hop, Afrofuturism, visual literacy, horror, the ethnogothic, and speculative design and its applications to visual rhetoric. Jennings is co-editor of the 2016 Eisner Award-winning collection *The Blacker the Ink: Constructions of Black Identity in Comics and Sequential Art* (Rutgers University Press, 2015) and co-founder/organizer of The Schomburg Center's Black Comic Book Festival in Harlem. He is co-founder and organizer of the MLK NorCal's Black Comix Arts Festival in San Francisco and SOL-CON: The Brown and Black Comix Expo at the Ohio State University.

Elaine Lopez

Elaine Lopez is a designer, artist, and educator. Her practice and research explore the intersection of culture, identity, equity, and Risograph printing within the design field. Her studio, LoPress Press, collaborates with cultural and academic institutions, including the Sachs Program for Arts Innovation at the University of Pennsylvania and the Center for Complexity at the Rhode Island School of Design, to give shape to research around culture and identity. She has lectured at IDEO, Samsung, Google, and academic institutions including the University of Pennsylvania, Texas State University, and Pratt Institute. She has presented at the Where Are the Black Designers? and In/Visible conferences. In 2019, she was awarded the AICAD Post-Graduate Teaching Fellowship at the Maryland Institute College of Art. She has served on the board of various design organizations, including AIGA Chicago and the Type Director's Club. She holds an MFA from the Rhode Island School of Design and a BFA from the University of Florida, both in graphic design. She is currently an assistant professor and the associate director of the

BFA in Communication Design program at Parsons School of Design in New York City.

Silvio Lorusso

Silvio Lorusso is a writer, artist, and designer based in Lisbon, Portugal. He is the author of *Entreprecariat* (Onomatopee, 2019) and *What Design Can't Do* (Set Margins', 2023). Lorusso is an assistant professor and co-director of the Center for Other Worlds at the Lusófona University in Lisbon, and a tutor in the Information Design program at the Design Academy Eindhoven. He holds a PhD in design sciences from the Iuav University of Venice. Lorusso's work touches upon visual communication, memes, post-digital publishing, entrepreneurship and precarity, digital platforms, design culture and politics, creative coding, art and design education, and videogames. His practice combines a variety of media such as video, website, artist's book, installation, and lecture. This activity is further stimulated by writing essays, curating exhibitions, and organizing public programs. Lorusso has been a member of Varia, the Center for Everyday Technology, as well as part of the editorial board of the Italian graphic design magazine, *Progetto Grafico*. Among other venues, his work has been presented at Het Nieuwe Instituut (Rotterdam), MaXXI (Rome), Transmediale (Berlin), The Photographers' Gallery (London), and Kunsthalle Wien. His writing has appeared in several magazines and publications, including *Volume*, *Real Life Magazine*, *Metropolis M*, *Esquire Italia*.

Maya Ober

Maya Ober is a designer, educator, researcher-turned-anthropologist. Her practice considers design and research as activist and socially transformative tools. Maya is currently a PhD candidate and lecturer at the Institute of Social Anthropology, University of Bern, in Switzerland. Her research focuses on feminist practices of design and design education from an engaged anthropological perspective. In 2017 Maya founded the activist platform, depatriachise design, and in 2020, she initiated the online directory feministcurricula.org, which maps and documents design educational initiatives that use feminist perspectives and pedagogies. As an educator Maya co-conceptualized the program Imagining Otherwise in 2018 and the Intersectional Lab in Arts and Design in 2022 at the Academy of Art and Design in Basel. Since 2021 Maya has co-directed Futuress – a feminist platform for design politics, a hybrid learning community and publishing platform.

Uzma Z. Rizvi

Uzma Z. Rizvi is an associate professor at Pratt Institute in Brooklyn, New York, and a visiting faculty at Shah Abdul Latif University in Khairpur, Pakistan. She received her PhD from the University of Pennsylvania (2007), followed by a postdoctoral fellowship at Stanford University (2008). She is the recipient of numerous fellowships and awards. Her publication record is similarly robust with books like *The Affect of Crafting* (2018); *Connections and Complexities: New Approaches to the Archaeology of South Asia* (2013); *The Handbook of Postcolonial Archaeology* (2010); and *Archaeology and the Postcolonial Critique* (2008). She is the principle investigator for the Laboratory for Integrated Archaeological Visualization and Heritage (LIAVH), an interdisciplinary, feminist, anticolonial, and antiracist space bringing together archaeological research with data management, visualization, and heritage practice, currently working at the UNESCO World Heritage Site of MohenjoDaro, Pakistan. Rizvi's work interweaves archaeology with cultural criticism, philosophy, critical theory, art, and design. With nearly two decades of work on decolonizing methodologies, intersectional and feminist strategies, and transdisciplinary approaches, her work has intentionally pushed disciplinary limits, and demanded ethical decolonial praxis at all levels of engagement, from teaching to research.

Kelly Walters

Kelly Walters is an artist, designer, and founder of the multidisciplinary design studio Bright Polka Dot. Her ongoing design research interrogates the complexities of identity formation, systems of value, and shared vernacular in and around Black visual culture. In 2021, Kelly was a Graham Foundation award recipient for her curated exhibition, *With a Cast of Colored Stars*. She is the author of *Black, Brown + Latinx Design Educators: Conversations on Design and Race* (Princeton Architectural Press, 2021) and the creative director and co-editor of *The Black Experience in Design: Identity, Expression & Reflection* (Allworth, 2022). Kelly is currently an assistant professor of communication design in Parsons School of Design at The New School in New York.

Lauren Williams

Lauren Williams is a Detroit-based designer, researcher, and educator. They work with visual and interactive media to understand, critique, and reimagine the ways social and economic systems distribute and exercise power over Black life and death. Through her creative practice and research, Lauren often investigates Blackness, identity, bodiliness, and social fictions to examine how racism is felt, embodied, and embedded within institutions. Themes of trust and the transformations enabled by social engagement shape both her approaches—collaboration, facilitation, collective production—and the questions she explores surrounding power and oppression, social relations, and social movements. She has taught design and interdisciplinary studios and intensives at the College for Creative Studies, ArtCenter College of Design, CalArts, and elsewhere. In the past, she has managed programs and policy aimed at cultivating economic justice at Prosperity Now in Washington, DC. Going forward, she is finding ways to align her capacities with revolutionary movements that build toward entirely different socioeconomic systems and usher in altogether new dimensions of power and freedom.

Colophon

Set Margins' #17
Through Witnessing: Threading the critiquing,
making, teaching of design

ISBN   978-90-833501-2-7

Editors   Nida Abdullah, Chris Lee, Xinyi Li

Contributing authors
Ahmed Ansari, Danielle Aubert,
Hayfaa Chalabi, John Jennings,
Silvio Lorusso, Elaine Lopez,
Maya Ober, Uzma Z. Rizvi,
Kelly Walters, Lauren Williams

Graphic design
Nida Abdullah, Chris Lee, Xinyi Li

Text editor
Rachel Valinsky

Printer
Printon, Tallinn, EE

Fonts
Mercure by Charles Mazé for Abyme;
Adobe Ming Std from Adobe;
HB Goblet A by HB Type

Made possible thanks to the generous support
of the Provost's Office for Strategic Initiatives
at the Pratt Institute.

Special thanks to Preston Thompson,
Ashna Kapadia, Sakura Tateiwa.

144

Set Margins'
setmargins.press